Creating a Success Culture

Transforming Our Schools
One Question at a Time

By Marjie Bowker
with Assistance from Liza Behrendt
and the Staff of Scriber Lake High School

Creating a Success Culture

Transforming Our Schools One Question at a Time

ISBN-13: 978-0-9908504-2-7

Cover Design by Jose Antonio Pulido

Cover Photo by Dan Bates/The Herald, of student Maize Phillips

Back Cover Art by Breanna Pratt

Book Layout by Hydra House

By Marjie Bowker

with Assistance from Liza Behrendt and the Staff of Scriber Lake High School

For more information, visit: http://www.edmonds.wednet.edu/slhs

*For all educators aspiring to create
heart and soul learning experiences on a daily basis.*

TABLE OF CONTENTS

FOREWORD

At the end of the summer of 2011, I was preparing for another productive year at Scriber Lake High School. We had many exciting things happening, and our staff was made up of individuals who were willing to do everything necessary to help our resilient students succeed.

In the back of my mind, however, I had always been searching for the piece that would make everything come together in a more positive way. That summer I received an email from Cal Crow asking if I would be available to meet to discuss a proposal. At that meeting I learned there was grant money available to help our students make better plans for their futures. Immediately I knew that Cal was someone who could help us with that missing piece.

I took his proposal to the staff and then to the district; both parties quickly granted approval to proceed. We did not know any specifics, but we were excited to learn more ways to help our students.

With the sizable grant we were awarded and through invaluable mentorship from Cal, we have made incredible progress in the last three years—all of which is documented in this book. I am very lucky to have had this opportunity and I look upon it as my best and most rewarding work.

Kathy Clift
Principal, Scriber Lake High School

When the right combination of people and events converge, wonderful (some say "magical") things can occur. This is what happened at Scriber Lake High School in Edmonds. The "magic" emerged from four sources:

1. A principal willing to risk and try something new
2. A creative, committed faculty and staff
3. The Center for Efficacy and Resiliency at Edmonds Community College, who wrote a proposal to create a success culture at Scriber Lake, and
4. College Spark Washington, who funded the proposal

This convergence resulted in *Your Future Now* (YFN), a project designed to increase the number of Scriber Lake students who graduate from high school and succeed in college.

English teacher Marjie Bowker drove the creation of this publication. Well-known for helping students write their stories, she willingly took on the task of helping Scriber adults do the same. She was assisted by teacher Liza Behrendt and nearly every other staff member.

This is not a "how to" manual; it is a collection of educators' and students' observations, 'heart and soul' experiences, and relationships that came together to change the Scriber Lake culture. It is compelling reading. Although no two readers will interpret these events in the same way, everyone should find at least one new idea to help create a student success culture.

We have not "arrived." Transformation is never complete. *Your Future Now* will always be a work in progress. Every new student or staff member–or policy directive from the state or district–will require new perspectives and behaviors.

Your Future Now has been a wonderful and productive ride, not only for Scriber but for the Center for Efficacy and Resiliency and for Edmonds Community College as a whole. The connections and benefits generated by this project were unimaginable three years ago.

If you would like to create something similar at your school, please let us know. College Spark is still looking for creative ways to improve student success and learning.

Your school could be next.

Cal Crow, Ph. D.

Director, Center for Efficacy and Resiliency

Edmonds Community College

20000 68th Avenue West

Lynnwood, Washington 98036-5999

425-640-1852

calcrow@edcc.edu

SCRIBER STAFF

Back row left to right: Greg Lange, Coleman Armstrong, Carol Bowman, Mike Carey, Andrea Hillman, Tammy Stapleton, Peter Folta, Cal Crow, Nate Seright, Dave Zwaschka, Leighanne Law. Middle row: Kanoe Vierra, Kathy Clift, Trinity Meriwood, Paula Lott, Richard Yi. Seated front: Marjie Bowker, Michael Waldren. Photo by Jacquie Lampignano

Left to right: Liza Behrendt, Paul Scott, Zach Taylor, Sondra Thornton, Brenna Hanson, Barb Kathol, Sarah Philley. Photo by Matt McCauley

Chapter One
HEART AND SOUL
Your Future Now—The Vision

How do we create a school with heart and soul, a place where every student wants to be?
We can't.

That's impossible.

Well, what if it *was* possible?

In the fall of 2011, the staff of Scriber Lake High School was challenged to do one thing: to imagine possibilities. Not to implement a curriculum or a system, but to grapple with questions regarding potential. Lots of questions.

Scriber is a public high school of approximately 250 students in the Edmonds School District, located just north of Seattle. We are one of Washington's oldest alternative schools. Ours is a school of choice; some students come to Scriber as freshmen, some come seeking a second chance and some land here for a last chance to graduate. The majority of Scriber students have struggled with homelessness, drugs and alcohol, depression, abuse, loss, or anxiety—and most have been failed by the system.

When our principal, Kathy Clift, asked if we were interested in working with someone to help create successful futures for our students, we had no reason to say no. We knew very little about Cal Crow—only that he had taught and consulted at many levels, including jails, prisons and children's psychiatric hospitals—and that he worked out of Edmonds Community College, located just a few miles from our campus. And that he wanted to work with us.

We were curious. When Cal began to present his philosophy over the course of the initial meetings, we liked what we heard.

More possibilities he asked us to imagine: What if we create a school that focuses more on students' dreams for the future than getting through a curriculum? What if we change student conversations from *transactions*– which often maintain the status quo–to *transformations*, where nothing stays the same?

During those meetings, Cal drew pictures on an old presentation flip board which he referred to as his "PowerPoint." One drawing showed two arrows: one pointed upward, labeled "Teacher," and one pointed sideways, labeled "Student."

"In the current system, our paths are not aligned," he said. "What we want, they are not buying." Then he drew another two arrows, both pointing upward. "How do we align what we offer with what students want? How do we create a culture where students and adults have the same mission—to ensure that all students become successful?"

Another flip board drawing: a figure with three parts, representing head, heart and soul. "Imagine a school where learning is viewed as an emotional and meaning-making event as well as a cognitive one," he said, "where curriculum is delivered in a way that generates a positive emotional charge and has meaning for the learner, where power moves from adults to students."

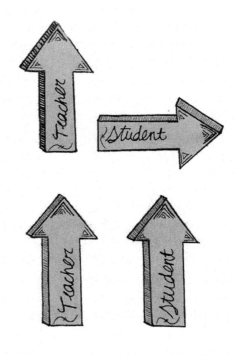

(Drawings by student Breanna Pratt)

 *head*

heart

soul

By this point we were hooked on the vision, but it sounded too good to be true. We wanted all of this, sure, but could we actually bring these ideals together within our system?

Cal also presented the four parts that form his philosophy for *Your Future Now*: research on self-efficacy, research on resiliency, the Appreciative Inquiry philosophy and the Motivational Interviewing technique. If we apply these four concepts as we develop our approach, he proposed, it will become a truly successful and highly collaborative effort.

And with that, we agreed to go on the questioning journey together.

THE FOUR GUIDING PRINCIPLES OF THE *YOUR FUTURE NOW* PHILOSOPHY

SELF-EFFICACY AND RESILIENCY

1. Self-Efficacy: The belief one has about his/her capability to perform a specific task or manage a situation.

Scriber's intention regarding student self-efficacy: Every student will acquire a belief that he/she has the capability to succeed in high school and to create a positive future. To ensure this will happen, we will:

    a. Create mastery experiences: Students will be given mastery experiences where they can be successful.
    b. Foster a sense of purpose: Staff will ensure that all students have a sense of the future and view Scriber as a place that will help them create a successful one.
    c. Expose students to role models: Students will be provided with examples of individuals similar to themselves who have created successful lives.
    d. Believe in each student: Staff members will make it clear that they believe in every student's capability to perform well in school and to create a successful future.

2. Resiliency: The ability to overcome obstacles and/or rebound from setbacks.

Scriber's intention regarding student resiliency: Every student will acquire the knowledge and skills necessary to overcome obstacles and rebound from setbacks. To ensure this will happen, we will:

    a. Be caring adults: Every student will be able to identify at least one personal "caring adult" at Scriber.
    b. Have high expectations: All students will have high expectations for themselves because adults will have high expectations for them.
    c. Provide opportunities to give voice: Every student will have a voice and an opportunity to contribute to something beyond him/herself.

QUESTIONING TECHNIQUES:

3. Appreciative Inquiry: The practice of highlighting and focusing on what you want to increase.

Scriber's Appreciative Inquiry intention: All students will be engaged in conversations that focus on their positive potential, strengthen belief in themselves and focus on solutions.

> **4. Motivational Interviewing: a directive, client-centered counseling style for eliciting behavior change by helping clients to explore and resolve ambivalence.**
>
> Scriber's Motivational Interviewing intention: All students will be engaged in conversations which emphasize listening, probing, reflecting and clarifying on the part of the adult in order to help them strengthen their readiness to change behaviors.
>
> How we aim to use these methods in our conversations:
>
> a. We want our conversations to be more about students' strengths, skills and talents, interests and dreams and less about curriculum and requirements.
>
> b. We want our conversations to be more about what students are learning, why that learning is important and how it might be useful to them in their futures.
>
> c. We want to learn as much about students as possible. The more we know about them, the wider the context we have for engaging them.
>
> d. We want to have more transformational, "heart and soul" conversations with students, and fewer "transactional" conversations that come mainly from the head.
>
> e. We want to spend less time giving information and more time probing and reflecting.

The Work Continues

Midway through this project, we became aware of the research regarding Adverse Childhood Experiences (The ACE Study) and many schools' attempts to reflect that research. For anyone familiar with The ACE Study, many of our approaches to implement trauma-informed and resilience-building practices will sound familiar, especially the pieces that focus on the importance of a caring adult in students' lives.

Our work with these concepts and strategies is ongoing. We, like most districts around the country, have had to deal with new educator evaluation systems, radical shifts in learning standards, greatly increased student testing and both planned and unexpected staff changes (four out of 13 teachers retired over the course of the grant implementation process). Continual change means continual adjustment, retraining, and rethinking of how to be most successful with our aims. We are by no means "there," and we hope our future evolutions will surpass what we have to offer now.

Still, this book was created because so many of Cal's proposals *do* work, and they work well. Scriber graduation rates have increased significantly, and more of our students are continuing their education after high school than ever before. Morale is noticeably higher among students and staff because we are creating a culture that promotes success in ways we hadn't before imagined. We are finding ways to brings students back into the center of their own education.

Even though we are still very much on this journey, we desired to take a snapshot of what we have developed so far and share it with other educators. Change is difficult, but our school culture did transform—by learning how to best question ourselves and our students, one question at a time.

Chapter Two

A MISSION STATEMENT WITH PURPOSE

Scriber Lake High School
will ensure
that all students become successful
by helping them identify, develop and maximize
their strengths, skills and talents.

Phones, hats, homework club, defiance. Rules—how do we get students to obey them? Every staff struggles with these issues, sometimes for hours on end without gaining any ground.

In the beginning of our *Your Future Now* meetings with Cal, we spent a lot of time asking how we could get students to obey the rules. Then we began to ask, "Why do we have all of these rules? What if we didn't need so many rules? What if we didn't have power struggles with students? What if we had parallel missions?"

Gradually, as we questioned how to get teacher arrows and student arrows pointing in the same direction (see illustration, Chapter One), we moved from asking "How do we 'fix' students so they will adhere to our culture?" to "How do we create a culture that draws students in, rather than creating power struggles?" (See Chapter Five on Appreciative Inquiry.)

One day Cal asked what our mission statement was. We looked at each other. Mission statement? We had no idea. Someone thought it might be on our letterhead. It was. We read it and realized why no one knew it; it was disjointed and lacked a purpose. Mission statements are supposed to drive you and state why your organization exists, but ours was serving neither goal. What if we were to rework it with the intention of aligning students' and teachers' goals?

A few staff members volunteered to tackle this problem and brought a draft to all of us for wordsmithing. The result was something we all believed in. We asked an artistic student to design a huge poster which we printed and laminated. We then placed one in each classroom and more in our hallways; we wanted to make it visible so the message would permeate our school. We began to talk about creating class norms *with* our students instead of *for* our students. Overall, our new mission statement became the touchstone used to guide the development of our school's culture.

STAFF REFLECTIONS

Andrea Hillman, Associate Principal

I was assigned as an administrator at Scriber in January of 2015 to help support the staff when Kathy Clift needed time away. One of the things that has resonated with me about the mission statement is that—in all my years of working in schools (15+)—I have never been in a school where the mission statement is more valued and more alive. It is at the core of the work staff does with kids every day.

It guides the purpose and objectives of the Steps to Success (S2S) curriculum and activities (see Chapter Ten). The activities are all shaped around having students identify their strengths and interests and how to capitalize on them to leverage their time here *right now*. As administrators, the mission statement guides conversations we have with students regarding the choices they are making and how those choices are helping them with their paths to success.

The mission statement also guides the curriculum we use with our students as they initiate into Scriber. They spend several weeks focused around three questions: 1) Who Am I? 2) What Do I Have to Declare? and 3) What Do I Need or How Am I Going to Get There?

Paula Lott, Family and Consumer Science

Having this colorful, student-developed poster with a variety of fonts placed at different angles draws everyone's attention to it. When the poster was first introduced, I had great discussions with my students about what it meant. When we set up classroom expectations at the beginning of the year, my classes took the mission statement as a starting guideline for what we do in class. This new statement is a positive improvement over the dry, bulleted wording of the former one.

Greg Lange, Student Transition Education Program (STEP)

Our new mission statement has caused me to further define success on a personal level–for my students and for myself.

Peter Folta, Social Studies

Our mission statement gives us a big license to push our students. When I read it to them before a difficult task, it makes them aware of my obligation to make them better–to push them out of their comfort zones. I am not really keen on "will ensure" because it is so concrete and definite, but it certainly holds us to a high standard.

Coley Armstrong, Entry, Learning Support and Social Studies

I use the mission statement every day with the new Entry students in an attempt to get them to think about whether their actions are helping them to be successful in school. Every time we have an issue in the classroom, I ask the student if the issue is helping with his or her success.

Richard Croxon, Science

The mission statement is more focused on career goals and encourages students to pursue their own ambitions.

Liza Behrendt, Leadership and Entry

Yesterday I talked with a student about self-doubt bordering on self-dislike or worse. I tried and tried to use the 17 Questions we've been working on (Chapter Five), but he kept redirecting toward negativity. Then I started talking about focusing on his strengths, skills and talents—a piece of our mission statement. I suggested that focusing on the positive things he brings could lead to him being able to give the gifts he has to give to the world, particularly as a teacher, which he hopes to someday become. He continued with some resistance, yet at some point we both realized that there was a breakthrough. There was a space of silence, both awkward and wonderful, after which he admitted in different words that this was healing. A positive transformation happened; it was subtle–a baby step–which was just right for that moment.

Nathan Seright, Social Studies

In our Catch-Up History Class we talked about how social studies skills help us in our everyday lives. I mentioned that we will focus on skills of inquiry, critical thinking and communication. The kids seemed interested in the idea that these skills will allow them to shape their ideas about the world and then help them implement the ideas to make a positive impact in their community. We also talked about some examples, such as discussing current events related to politics, forming an idea about our beliefs and then voting for someone who represents us.

Trinity Meriwood, Business Education and Graphic Arts

As someone with a marketing background, I am a big fan of well thought-out mission statements. Ours is simple; it includes *everyone*, from staff to students. It is *relevant*, so it can be looked at and not just dismissed as frivolous. And I heard that the poster was student designed, which, in my opinion, always leads to actual interest from the students. It gives them an attachment and ownership.

Chapter Three
WHAT, WHY, HOW?
Extending the Learning Target

As a staff, we aim to help students make connections between their efforts at school and the realization of their dreams for the future. Our mission statement is to ensure that all students become successful by helping them identify, develop, and maximize their strengths, skills, and talents. Therefore, we take seriously the classic student questions, "Why do we have to do this?" and, "What's the point?" If there are no good answers, then right, why teach it? If our content does not support students' goals and dreams in some way, why should they learn it? In those cases, something needs to be adjusted.

Of course our conviction is that the learning we offer *is* meaningful. Still, if students do not embrace that notion, they will not apply themselves. On the other hand, if students understand how important their learning is, they will try hard and produce their best work. That leads to mastery experiences, which builds students' belief in themselves and a foundation of skills for a successful future.

In order to support self-efficacy along these lines, we practice asking students to identify and express what is meaningful about their learning. This chapter shares one particular method of doing so called, "What, Why, How?"

The format is simple. Teachers ask students these three questions:

What are we learning?
Why are we learning it?
How will we use this knowledge now or in the future?

A collection of "What, Why, How?" conversations and reflections follow. Although not all student responses reflect a sense of importance in learning, rich dialogue has arisen out of this approach. While a teacher-specified, single learning target stated at the beginning of the class may help focus on the "What," asking "Why? and How?" invites critical thinking and a diversity of valid viewpoints. Significant, higher-level thinking and greater student engagement are cultivated and we as educators gain inspiration for keeping our teaching relevant to those we serve.

Subject: English
Teacher: Dave Zwaschka
Grade level(s): 11th and 12th
Learning Activity: My junior/senior English classes are beginning *Enrique's Journey* by Sonia Nazario this week.
Timing: We just finished the prologue and first two chapters and have discussed some issues surrounding life in Honduras and immigration.
Collection Method: Students wrote responses first and then we discussed as a class.

Q: What are we learning this week?
- We are learning about how even when you don't have much, your perseverance and desire can still make things possible.
- What it is like for the families in Honduras whose parents leave the children alone and have to take the chance of being attacked or worse just so they can bring money and make a better life for their children.
- We are learning about the importance of using sensory details in writing.
- To put ourselves into the settings of the stories we read.

Q: Why are we learning this?

- To use our five senses in a story, so that it could help us be more detailed in our own personal narratives. And we are learning about the hardships of Enrique, Enrique's mom, and Honduras so we can understand what life is like for everyone in Honduras and those that come to America by riding on top of a train.
- So we know what's going on in the world, and what people go through. I think we should be grateful for what we have because people risk their lives to come to America.
- To develop and build connections.
- I think we are learning this to understand that we are all humans and to treat each other equally. It's the common humanity we share. People are cruel and kind—it's like Lourdes's bosses: some make lunch for her, others make her kneel on the floor to scrub their floors. A guy gets on a public bus and he needs to get to work but doesn't have bus fare. He says to the driver, "I need to get to my job, but I don't have the money to pay you." The driver says, "That's okay, get on, I'll take you." That driver sees the humanity in the man, he understands they are both people.
- It motivates us to help those in need.
- It's a story about us young people.
- I'm not sure.
- Because people aren't treated right and this is a hot discussion. Hopefully, future human rights will let everyone go everywhere.

Q: How will learning about this help you with your future goals and plans?

- I have no idea.
- What we are learning might help me by having knowledge of what happens to immigrants, and to be more thankful.
- You could get a job or volunteer to help these people have a better life.
- To grow, to help our community make a better living.
- By seeing different points of view, to dive into the diverse.
- To not have preconceived notions or prejudices.
- Throughout our whole lives we have to be empathetic and create connections.
- My future goals and plans have nothing to do with what I learned in class this week. (I want to be a chef.)
- Not to judge. You never know someone's back story.
- It will be my motivation not to live my life in poverty.
- I think this book will give me more insight into the dangers others face every day and to write with picture-painting descriptions.

Reflection

I hesitated a long time before asking my students the three questions and approached this discussion with some discomfort. I've always hoped my activities and projects were engaging and purposeful, but rarely have I asked my students to reflect upon questions such as these. I was fearful that, offered the opportunity to reflect in this manner, my students would be at a loss to answer—mostly because I had failed to make reflecting upon these questions part of the daily classroom culture.

Many responses were thoughtful, some more than that. The student's comment about the bus driver in particular transcended the book to relate the theme of human connection to his own experience. He shared it in class (I wrote while he spoke), and upon finishing sat quietly looking at his desk. The entire class sat quietly, too, taking in what they had just heard. Several students whispered, "That was so cool, what you just said," "Wow," and" Awesome." Not only did we all benefit from such an insightful and personal reflection, but this student did, too.

I'm glad I finally asked my classes these questions. Doing so pointed to some areas of improvement for me, but also affirmed my hopes that the book, and the larger immigration discussion, has held meaning and purpose for my students. There was less to be afraid of than I thought.

Subject: Economics /Specifically: How Companies Work

Teacher: Peter Folta

Grade level(s): 11-12

Learning Activity: This reflection was a part of a unit on corporations—how they work, how they make profit, and how they adapt. All students had completed research on a corporation (or a company), and presented a PowerPoint on that company. Additionally, all students played an online stock-market simulation during which they followed and monitored a portfolio of company stocks.

Timing: At the end of the two-week unit.

Collection Method: Discussion.

Q: What are you learning?

- We are learning about stock markets and how stocks are always moving. About how you want to sell when stocks are up and we are also learning about the build-up to the Great Depression.
- Global economies, companies and their successes and failures.
- What makes a company strive, technology and how it affects our future.
- Stock Market: How it works, the Crash of 1929.

Q: Why are we learning it?

- To understand how a business is operated and started, and how they have changed.
- So I'm not ignorant.
- To increase our knowledge of what is going on around us, so we can retire someday, to learn about value, to become more knowledgeable business-wise.
- To better our knowledge on what our futures might look like.
- We can be able to tell how a company is successful not just by looking at their stocks.
- So we can possibly buy ourselves some stocks to make money for our futures.

Q: How can I use this knowledge now or in the future?

- I can use this in the future because by having a better understanding of the stock market (and how it works) we can or will be better able to know how to use it and how to read from it.
- I can use this information to potentially help me decide what I want to study after high school (or maybe I don't want to study it).
- To sound more intelligent.
- To understand how your present or future workplace works.
- I can use any of this information for future jobs, schooling or when my grandchildren ask.
- I could use this information to help me invest my money (stocks!) or start my own business.
- If I ever thought about retiring early, maybe investing in the right company, the right stocks could get me there sooner. It is either you win or you lose sometimes, but investing in the right company might get you a new car.
- Knowing businesses could help me start my own if I ever wanted to.

Reflection

My impression is that the students felt this was a worthwhile unit and useful to learn. The stock market simulation was emotional for many of them, as they gained and lost fictitious money. Researching a company of their choice produced varying results, but I did come to learn that those interested in business really dove into the project.

I believe that I could use the "What, Why, How?" questions more frequently as a way to monitor my objectives. In a sense this is really a decent survey or even an assessment. I think in some cases I need to be more explicit with reasons for learning early in a unit of study; perhaps I need to scaffold this more. This will serve me well as I continue to improve as a teacher. This all takes me back to graduate school 14 years ago and I appreciate that aspect of it.

Subject: Leadership
Teacher: Liza Behrendt
Grade level(s): 10-12
Learning Activity: Project to provide donated items to people in Seattle who are homeless (multi-day project), on a day when we had realized we had several obstacles to overcome before the actual trip to Seattle.
Timing: Near the end of the project planning phase.
Collection Method: Journal writing

Q: What have we learned?

- How to transform leadership into an everyday experience.
- We can make change; we can make a difference, even if it is just handing out donations to a handful of people.
- New skills—better communication skills, publicity, calling people over the phone, trying to get everyone involved and focused on what needs to be done.
- Learn from our mistakes or even from procrastination. We as a class are sometimes off task, but it's important to learn from that and do better.
- We're learning how to be compassionate, caring, helpful people; not to judge people because you never know what others have been through.
- How to ask for help.
- This teaches us not to be self-centered; when there are people dying on the streets, cold at night, it makes you appreciate your bed and extra blanket forever.
- How to decide on things without having people be mad at each other in disagreements.

Q: Why are we learning it?

- To become better leaders so we can be more successful in leadership roles. Everything we are learning ties in to leadership in some way or another, and is helping us gain those skills.
- How to organize projects so we can take them into our own hands in the future.
- Organizing a project like this takes a lot of work and dedication. Doing this project I've done things I was always terrified of doing before leadership (calling people over the phone or making announcements over the loudspeaker).
- To know how to overcome problems.
- Not only better ourselves, but also to better us as a leader because a good leader has all these traits (compassionate, caring, helpful).
- Kindness, no matter how small, will go a long way in life, and there needs to be more of it. Hopefully people will see what we do, and we can lead them by example.
- It seems like we all love seeing others happy and helping them before ourselves.
- I grew up being told if I gave a homeless person money they would just spend it on drugs, but seeing how

clothes, shoes and food makes such a difference and lights up their worlds makes me feel different.

- It may seem like this is all just "fun," all just "community service," but going out and wanting to help others and feeling good for doing it and doing what it takes to help others takes leadership and confidence. People say going and doing community service can help with depression and that says a lot; when you're helping it makes you feel good.

Q: How will we use this knowledge now or in the future?

- Help us make Scriber a better place.
- Help us be better leaders in work industries, volunteering, and being better parents; the skills we're learning will help us in jobs, careers and college.
- I could help my community other than just the homeless.
- We learn new things about ourselves each day we move forward with the project.
- Forever—I think we should help other people who need help.
- I can use this knowledge to better myself and help others both now and in the future; we can use these skills forever because we have now learned and practiced them.
- The main reason I feel like we're doing this is so we can lead others.
- Not everyone has it good like me. I need to be thankful for the life I have.
- Using this knowledge now could help me make each day a little bit brighter.

Reflection

We did this as a journal activity, so I was easily able to capture exact words from students. The trip to Seattle went well overall, and the learning continued along the way. I'm a strong believer in experiential learning, and we keep the class as democratic as possible with a great deal of group decision-making. This combined pedagogy has its downsides, yet the vibrant learning evident in these reflections gives me a renewed sense of conviction about developing ways for students to be in the lead in this class... and in life.

Subject: English

Teacher: Leighanne Law

Grade level(s): 10-12

Learning Activity: Debating controversial issues in current events

Timing: This discussion fell toward the end of a three week debate unit.

Collection Method: Students took a Google Form survey, then I read the results out loud.

Q: What have you learned about yourself, classmates, or the world in our debate unit?

- People are very opinionated and passionate.
- That my classmates enjoy arguing a lot and also, I'm only good at debating if it's a topic I care about.
- I get really mad really fast. I thought I was the Switzerland of our class—turns out I'm super opinionated and hate it when people disagree.
- I am terrible at debating
- I'm a very heated debater. When I feel strongly about something, I fight to prove my point until I feel like I've made my point.
- I haven't learned anything.

Q: Why are we learning how to debate/argue/discuss?

- I am not quite sure. Maybe because knowing how to debate/argue is an important skill to have.
- Everyone gets in an argument sometime in their lives; may as well win it, right?

- It helps us to better our thought processes and it helps us learn how to express our opinions to others in an intellectual way.
- Debating is the essence of all arguments. If two people disagree on something, they debate, and people disagree all the time.
- Researching and being able to talk about a subject is a very important skill.
- The importance of being able to argue, is usually getting your way. Things are easier to do if you can defend "your side" adequately.

Q: How can I use this knowledge now or in the future?

- I will be able to *school* my brother so hard whenever he disagrees with me.
- I've gained nothing.
- Confuse people to the point of where they're agreeing with me. Which will be fantastic. Also if I do become a lawyer, it will help form cases and give me perspective.
- In a debate, at work, online discussions.
- If someone asks a question about a certain topic, I can fight for both sides of it and be able to explain how I feel in a professional way.
- Well for one, I know that to argue a point, you need facts to back up your claims. I could use this information in the future when looking for a job, etc...

Reflection

Each English class begins with ten minutes of journal writing followed by a share out. This routine has done wonders for our small class in terms of a positive classroom culture and a welcoming sense of community. We have been using Chromebooks and Google Apps for Education to promote 21st Century skills, research, critical thinking, and sharing, so when I asked the students to take an online survey to reflect on the debate unit we just finished, they had no trouble navigating the websites or being completely honest in their reflections. They had around ten minutes to complete the form and then I showed their anonymous responses on the big screen and read them aloud.

One thing teaching this unit has shown me is that when students have a say in what, how and why they learn, they take ownership of their education. For me, this goes beyond participation and engagement. I often ask for student input into the topics we discuss and the strategies we use. This has led to some incredibly dynamic and passionate debates in which the students plead for more time to research the topic, come to me before or after class with ideas for discussion, and stay past the bell at the end of the day to finish their debates.

Another thing I have noticed is that the students' ownership of this unit has transformed them. Shy students who have never been comfortable speaking in public are arguing passionately for their side with strong evidence and strong voices. Passionate students who have only wanted to hear their side now wait patiently for others to speak and are able to build on their ideas.

Subject: Graphic Arts

Teacher: Trinity Meriwood

Grade level(s): 9-12

Learning Activity: Explore Adobe Illustrator

Collection Method: Discussion

Q: What are we learning?

- How to use Adobe Illustrator to manipulate/customize fonts.

Q: Why are we learning it?

- To make unique fonts.
- In order to be able to create custom logos (along with using Photoshop, if necessary).
- We can use it to create media.
- It's cool.

Q: How will we use this knowledge now or in the future?

- To create personal logos (if you're in a band or a DJ, you will need a logo).
- If we consider doing graphic design as a profession.

Subject: Algebra
Teacher: Richard Yi
Collection Method: Wrote the questions on the board, students wrote responses on paper. Some students were curious to learn of results, so teacher showed the typed responses via SmartBoard and students read them.

Q: What have we learned?

- Algebra

Q: Why are we learning it?

- Accounting doesn't do itself.
- We're learning it mostly to play out this high school and college game.
- We are learning this because we may need to know it someday and it's always good to learn even if it won't need it.
- Because some of us might need it for jobs and it looks good on a college application and so we aren't stupid.
- So we can be well-rounded in the area of math.
- We are learning algebra because like any other class, it's required for you to graduate. Also, we need to know the information so we are ready for adulthood.
- I know in the future we will need some sort of math, algebra, or geometry. So we can know how to do things because mostly everything in life is used by these three things.
- I think we are learning it because it may help us in the future.

Q: How will we use this knowledge now or in the future?

- You need algebra skills to program, get a job in the big business industry, or to just do your taxes.
- Yes, in certain successful jobs you need algebra, but most jobs? No, you really only need the basics. I use this knowledge to graduate.
- You can use it by figuring out what you would need to combine chemicals together to make certain foods, drinks, inventions, and etc.
- You can use it for your job and or business. Even if you were a common criminal you would use algebra, so that's why.
- I'm going to be an engineer so it's going to be needed for a lot of measuring.
- I don't think it would help me any by knowing it now, like we only have to know it because some jobs require it!

Subject: English

Teacher: Marjie Bowker

Grade level(s): 9

Learning Activity: Reading Steinbeck's *Of Mice and Men*.

Timing: This discussion took place on the day we finished the novel.

Collection Method: Projected each question, one at a time, with the document camera and wrote down answers as they were offered by students.

Q: What did we learn?

- We read the novel *Of Mice and Men* by John Steinbeck.
- We learned about the Great Depression during the 30's.
- We worked on writing structured paragraphs and using evidence from the text to support a main idea.

Q: Why did we learn this?

- So we could become better readers and writers.
- So we could have an example of good descriptions and dialogue in writing.
- So we wouldn't be afraid to kill off a character if it needed to happen for the big picture.
- Because the book shows how important dreams are.
- Because the book shows how racism was back then, that it has always been around.
- Because you can't have bad without good.
- So that we could see how it was to live during that time.
- Because all of us treat people badly at times and we can see that in the characters.

Q: How will we use this knowledge now or in the future? What are the truths about ourselves that this book reveals?

- That it's important to give people freedom. That confinement is never good for the soul.
- Makes us aware of people with special needs and how hard it is to be patient at times.
- That it's possible to find joy in every situation, that having dreams is really important for all people.
- That if you work too hard you won't have happiness.
- That everyone has a story and that all people are lonely in some way.
- It helps you grow and move forward after hardships knowing that others have done this.
- It stimulates your brain in a good way to keep it "exercised."
- It allows you to understand someone else and to think about how to treat people who have less power than you do.
- It makes us smart and we can discuss this book with other people in the future.

Reflection

My class really enjoyed this conversation and a few even commented that they felt they knew *Of Mice and Men* better than other 9th graders in the district. They felt very connected to it and wanted to show off their knowledge in some kind of competition.

I felt insecure about inviting these discussions at first. I worried that the questions might open up a negative forum for my students to declare everything we did to be meaningless. However, the opposite has occurred; I find that we usually solidify our sense of purpose as a class when we take discussions to this level.

Now I often tell my students that they should be able to ask these questions of me—and be able to answer them on their own—at any time. I hold the discussion at different times during my units, depending on when I think it will be most useful. Overall, this process has challenged me to always think about the importance of what I am teaching and how to articulate its relevance; if I can't do that, then I probably shouldn't be teaching it.

Subject: Competency Based Learning (CBL)
Teacher: Sarah Philley
Grade level(s): 10-12
Learning Activity: Various (World History 9 & 10, WA State History, English 11, Algebra 1)
Timing: Midway through the quarter.
Collection Method: Students were asked questions via a worksheet and responded in written form.

Q: What have we learned?

- **Skills for Success:** To set and accomplish goals. To push myself further with perseverance. To accomplish a life goal (reading Frankenstein). Time management. Prioritizing. About my own religion. Work ethic. Self-discipline. Organization. That I like to work on my own. Responsibility. To push myself to learn and better understand Algebra—I am proud of this accomplishment because math has been a real struggle for me in the past.
- **Academic/Study Skills:** Grammar errors and how to fix them. Analyzing literature for bias. Formatting for a variety of essays. Better problem solving skills. How a summary compares to an analysis.
- **Understanding Our World:** WWII and the Cold War ("I've learned a lot more about WWII than I knew before," and "I'm learning right now about the Cold War and Space Race between both the Superpowers U.S. and the Soviet Union"). The Holocaust. Africa (Nelson Mandela, Rwanda Genocide, "I've learned that in some parts of Africa there are families dying from sickness that can be treated but they don't have the resources"). Religions (The Tibetan book of the dead, Life of Buddha, "How all gods are looked at differently," "What people around the world think of religion," and "How religion affected our world"). I've learned that fixing problems in a nation that is falling apart can be difficult. How different areas of Washington have different climates and how that affects things. Our country's/state's history. About government. Culture in Washington.

Q: Why are we learning it?

- **Immediate Needs:** To help me get caught up. To get credits. To prepare me for the yearly Algebra exam. To graduate.
- **Intrinsic Motivation & Personal Growth:** To prove to myself I can finish what I start. To become wiser and more knowledgeable. To learn more about what I believe in. To help me be independent. So I can know about consciousness (spirituality). To humble myself. To help me understand about others' lifestyles.

Q: How will we use this knowledge now or in the future?

- **Education:** To build critical thinking skills. To expand education and knowledge. To use this knowledge to go further in life. To take harder classes involving religion. To enhance my writing skills.
- **Job:** If I become a video game designer I need to be able to analyze something and give my input. Later this could help me because I now know that I like to work on my own. To make money and gain a better occupation. To be punctual when I need to be. To have a successful job and life. Knowing how Algebra works can be a good thing when I get a job that requires these skills. To help me get a job involving religious history.
- **Personal Development:** It gives me something to think about and see where I really want to take myself in the very near future. We can be more successful by making better decisions like picking and

choosing responsibilities over procrastinating. When trying to persuade someone or be more valid in a religious argument. To be a better me. To have a successful life and be motivated. In learning about all the problems a nation may have I've realized how lucky I am to be in America. So I know how to write correctly. To be able to analyze and give my best interpretation. Because it's important to know how numbers work. To use it on my kids.

- **World Outside of Self:** People can learn from the mistakes of history. Everyone should be educated about our country's history and accomplishments. Understanding the importance of government regulations. To know what actually goes on and have the information to back it up. To better understand all of the counties in Washington. To influence the area I live in. To talk about another's religion with them. To pass down my knowledge of WWII and teach others how bad it was. I now appreciate doctors and medicine more and am more willing to try and help the people in Africa as much as I can. To be grateful. Learning about sickness and death in Africa made me reflect more on what I already have. When I was fixing the problems in my nation (project), I learned how many more problems there are under the surface.

Reflection:

The Competency Based Learning course model is a closely monitored, independent study class with one-on-one teacher support. The nature of the class cultivates an environment of personal ownership toward the learning process. This exercise provided a wonderful opportunity for students to connect what they were learning to a broader perspective of transferrable skills for life beyond the classroom, which came very naturally for all of the students surveyed.

I am curious to know what the responses would have been if we had asked the same questions prior to our work with *Your Future Now*. Based on the positive outcomes of this exercise, I will continue utilizing it as a reflective assessment within Competency Based Learning.

Andrea Hillman, Associate Principal

I have experienced an 'aha' moment regarding the use of learning targets. Every educational practitioner knows it makes sound educational sense to provide students with a learning objective for the day, week, unit, year, etc., and opportunities for them to have some closure on that learning target by simply looping back to it at the end of a lesson and checking in on whether or not they got there in a day. Those are easy. The piece this grant work has augmented is to not only share the learning target, but to share the reason for the learning and to provide students with the opportunity to talk about how the learning can impact them and their futures in a positive way right now. "What, Why, How?" is the 'missing link' to providing the context and the relevancy that disengaged learners need so much.

Chapter Four

CHANGING CONVERSATIONS, PART ONE

Envisioning a Future

It is a bold step, especially for a young person, to envision a future that incorporates one's interests, even passions. Envisioning a fulfilling future requires a platform of self-efficacy. Self-efficacy—our belief in our capability to perform a task or manage a situation—is often described as the single greatest predictor of success in school and work. Students do well because they believe they can do well and expect they will do so. Numerous studies have shown the relationship between "belief in capability" and aspirations. Students who have goals, plans and a reason for being in school—in other words, students who can envision a future—have a higher sense of self-efficacy than students who focus on meeting requirements, earning credits and just doing what it takes to get through the system.

Large numbers of students in alternative education programs do not believe they could ever be "good students." They flirt with dropping out because the work feels too hard or because they don't see any use in what they are learning. Or perhaps they stay in school and rely primarily on adults to "get them through." Our goal with the career planning element of the *Your Future Now* project (many of them included in Chapter Ten) is to help every student acquire a sense of the future. The following conversations are examples of ways we engaged students to get their thought processes directed in this way..

Kathy Clift, Principal

My transformation as a principal has had an extraordinary impact on my interactions with students. Because I have changed the focus of my conversations, the way I think about students is completely different. Now I see clearly that graduation and earning credits isn't the big deal, it's the whole life dream that is. The way we treat students at Scriber has changed through making connections; knowing their stories has allowed us to see them in a truer light.

As a result, suspensions have gone way down. I used to suspend kids for not attending an after- school homework club (for those who were not passing all of their classes), but began to see this as counter-productive. Suspending them was just one more way of telling them they weren't good enough. The only reasons I suspend kids now are for drugs and weapons; otherwise, I just change the conversation to focus on their stories or dreams. I find out what is really going on. I ask them how their behavior is helping them to get where they are going and try to build a relationship of trust with them.

Here are a few conversations I have had with students where everything changed with just one question about their future:

One student was going to beat up another student with brass knuckles. If that didn't work, she planned to shoot her. This was written in a text message, so I was required by law to "Emergency Expel" her. I called her down to have this discussion and told her I had proof that she sent a text stating that she was planning to hurt someone.

She described the situation with nonchalance and admitted her intention to beat up the other student.

"I can't have you at school if I'm not sure you are safe," I said. As she continued to justify her anger, I looked up her discipline record (judging her for her words, tone and appearance as I did so) and saw that she had only earned .75 of one credit as a sophomore.

When I finally had a moment to speak, I said, "I see that you have less than one credit right now. I'm wondering, **what is it you plan to do in your future?**"

With this one question, I saw a complete change come over her. Her body language relaxed as she answered, "I want to do something in the vet field. I love animals."

In that moment, my judgment turned to interest and suddenly we were involved in a conversation about her passion, the discipline issue forgotten. I also asked her what she knew about pursuing this field and found out that she knew little. Still, her excitement was evident.

"Well, we need to get this discipline stuff behind you so that you can focus on your dreams," I said.

No part of the tough girl remained at that point. She had become trusting and conversational.

A little while later, her mother came in for the required expulsion meeting.

"I'm going to have to emergency expel your daughter, but when we are sure that the other kids at this school are safe, we will bring her back to she can get to more important things," I said. "Your daughter has some dreams we need to work on."

Her mother—who was obviously used to discussing her daughter's troubles—relaxed, too. She smiled at the mention of her daughter's dreams, and was relieved to be discussing something other than behavior.

Both mother and daughter left the office feeling happy, their resentment and anger fading, replaced by the positive interaction.

I called another student down one afternoon because he had been skipping his classes after lunch. He was also familiar with discussing behavior problems.

"You're not in trouble. I am not suspending you," I said. "But I do want you to know this: I'm treating you differently. I know you need different things, and I will give that to you. But in return, I need your honesty. I need to know if you aren't going to attend after lunch so that we can put you in the classes you'll attend."

He agreed.

"And one other thing...**what is it you plan to do in your future?**"

"You won't like it," he said, and smiled. "I want to be in research for medical marijuana."

I made a pantomime of writing and said, "Medical field."

He laughed, then went on to explain that his grandmother had cancer, and that his passion was to find a way to make her suffering less severe.

"That's valid. I know you love her," I said, and our conversation, once again, moved away from the realm of negative behavior to a discussion full of meaning. Suddenly the conversation was about heart and soul.

Another student had not followed through with his drug and alcohol contract. Before—when I wasn't focusing on kids' dreams—I would have told him, "You're going to STEP (a program for struggling students). You didn't follow the contract." I would have been authoritarian about it and he would have been mad and horrified, leaving no chance for a positive conversation.

Instead, I opened by saying, "Things aren't going too well. You haven't shown up to your drug and alcohol meetings. Why?"

He answered that he hated the meetings and wouldn't go, no matter what. This is when I asked him, "**Now, what is it you plan to do in your future?**" He told me how interested he was in the medical field. He was very passionate while explaining it.

I answered, "I'm not supposed to let you back in school because of your violation, but I see a lot of potential in you and I want to do what is best for you here. Tell me, what should I expect of you?"

He then told me that he was no longer using at all. "I realized that drugs were getting in my way, and now I don't want to get thrown off track," he said.

I asked him if he would agree to a random UA sometime in the next three weeks.

"No trouble at all. Any time," he answered.

Again, this conversation about his future changed a potentially tense, negative conversation into one that encouraged and invited trust.

Tammy Stapleton, Student Transition Education Program (STEP)

Every day at lunch while I monitor the parking lot area, I talk to students outside of the gym. One student in particular often walks over and speaks to me. At one point, he was a very difficult student who refused to do work and had frequent violent outbursts. Now he is talking positively and is very focused on his future. Recently, he told me he knew he used to be a "pain" but has realized how wrong he was.

One day **I asked him how he made the choice to turn things around**. First he described how much pain he used to experience because of a car accident, which had made focusing in school very difficult. Along with that pain subsiding, people had started talking to him as if he could do things. In the past people had typically spoken to him in terms of what he could not do; they seemed focused on limitations, so he also focused on limitations.

He said that was "a very frustrating way to look at things." **When our staff started asking him questions like he had no limitations, only choices**, it made him look at school and everything differently.

This student has changed his IEP status so that he no longer has emotional/behavioral goals and is now in the Entry program (before he was part of the Intensive Learning Support (ILS) program). He is currently passing his Scriber classes and is also in my Competency Based Learning (CBL) class where he is dividing his time between working on credit retrieval and studying to take the SAT.

He plans to graduate on time in 2016 and is hoping to go to college on a football scholarship; however, he plans to go with or without a scholarship.

Coley Armstrong, Social Studies and Entry

Last spring I had a conversation with a student about her future. She had been removed from one of her other classes and was wandering the campus when I showed up for my class. She was mad because she felt she was never going to amount to much.

I asked her what her goals or dreams were. She reported that she would like to own a small business or salon, or become an actress. She was upset because of changes in her personal life that she felt made her dreams unattainable.

I asked her why the change made her feel that way (**say more about that…**). She said there was no way she could open her business or act now. I asked her how old she thought most small business owners or actresses are when they begin to make it. She said 22. I said that a lot of people do not begin to have success until they are approaching 30, or even later.

She began to realize that she needed to plan for beyond high school by more than a couple of years and that success takes time. She ended the conversation by saying that she would try harder for the remainder of the school year.

Trinity Meriwood, Business Education and Graphic Arts

Last week I discovered that one of my Family students and I had more in common than I thought. He's someone I don't see every day, so we don't have as many chances to discuss today, tomorrow or the future. But when we started to talk about soccer, I learned that he's also a goalkeeper. The first words out of my mouth were, "We're so rare, we're like unicorns. You have a *strong* chance to play at the next level. Did you know that?"

He really didn't. He was too busy to play on a recreational team and could only play for a school team. He didn't know about being recruited or that most community colleges have room for goalkeepers. He didn't know he could likely get scholarship money. **We had a good conversation about some things he could do to make this happen**, and now I have more reasons to bug him when he checks in.

Richard Yi, Math

In preparation for our Futures Fair, a student in my Family and I **began a discussion about her future**. She expressed her interest in becoming a high school math/science teacher. We talked about some of the universities and colleges represented on our campus that day and started making a list of questions to ask. We came up with several questions including tuition costs, programs offered, and dormitory life. As I was wrote the questions on my white board, she wrote them down on an index card. When Family was over, she headed over to the college presentation full of excitement.

Sondra Thornton, paraeducator, Intensive Learning Support

A student who has been in a juvenile correctional institution—and who has also grappled with learning challenges—came to Scriber earlier this year. Initially he presented a great deal of defensiveness.

I came to him and said (in the language he used), "I want you to know that there are people here who you can trust, people who are genuinely on your side. We're not the police "coming at you." We may seem to be coming at you, but **we're working with you to help you make progress into your future."**

He looked at me in a really funny way.

I continued, "Sometimes there are times when we're going to ask you to stop something you're doing, but we're going to explain to you why we're giving that direction, **to help you continue to move forward in your journey."**

That conversation marked a breakthrough. He came to me later in the day and apologized. We ended up talking and sharing deeply for a half an hour. That was huge! I don't know about touching his heart, but he sure as heck touched mine.

We still have our moments, he and I, but I tell myself, "Remember he is learning this, remember where he's coming from, don't give up on him."

Michael Waldren, Science paraeducator

During my brief tenure at Scriber, no student has conveyed disinterest in school more highly than T. I attempted **asking him a few questions regarding his future** and how he felt about his progress. His responses seemed to be temporary distractions from his struggle for productivity.

To make matters worse, he also reiterated multiple times that he had no interest in science, and that there was nothing within the subject that could motivate him. Given all my observations, it certainly appeared that his mind was far away from scientific studies.

A shift in this behavior came completely out of nowhere. One morning, during supervision duties in the cafeteria, I overheard an animated conversation between this student and one of his peers over whether or not certain compounds could vaporize flesh. He and the other student were exchanging names of chemical compounds and discussing their destructive qualities. I was completely baffled.

I waited until the debate was over to approach him. I **asked him to expand** on his interest regarding dangerous chemical compounds, then mentioned the interconnectedness of all scientific subjects. With this revelation, the relevancy of science resonated with him.

He is still working on his road to success in science, but he now has motivation to push forward. When he was having difficulty picking an element for a project, I initiated a conversation with him regarding the highly reactive properties of uranium, and he was all set.

Zach Taylor, College and Career Specialist

As I walk through the halls of Scriber, one thing I constantly hear from students is "we need to talk." Often, these words are associated with something negative. However, these are magical words for me. At Scriber, when students say "We need to talk," it almost always indicates a necessary **discussion about the future.**

In our mission statement, we ensure success for *all* students. I have dealt with convicted felons, a former student who was not allowed on campus (he trespassed so he could work on his future), and 20 year-old students with "freshman" credits. No child is ever written off. Students who have already graduated come in to seek information on scholarships or colleges. When the class of 2015 graduates, most—if not all—will have a plan for after graduation, and most will have already taken steps toward that goal.

One of my favorite moments of the year was when I had four different parents in my office at the same time, all helping their kids complete FAFSA (federal student aid) applications. This was not a planned event; I had not contacted any of the parents. Our students now constantly pester their parents or guardians to come in to fill out applications for grants and financial aid. Students are starting to take ownership of their future, and parents often express "shock" to learn of their child's interest in college.

The most damaging message passed on from parents, media, or other adults is that "you can't afford to go to college." This message is simply wrong. For most disadvantaged students, federal student aid will cover most—if not all—of the cost of school. I try to get our students to understand that they *can* afford college and then hope that realization changes their views on the future. The second challenge is to inform students about what a post-secondary education is. While a student may not thrive as a high school student, there are thousands of different pathways for education post high school—one to fit each student's learning style, hopes and dreams.

Chapter Five
CHANGING CONVERSATIONS, PART TWO
Appreciative Inquiry

In addition to shifting discussions toward successful futures, what if we had oh, say, 17 carefully crafted questions—based on Appreciative Inquiry and Motivational Interviewing—that we could use in our conversations with students to strengthen their positive potential?

The 17 Questions listed below were given to us at the outset by Cal. He designed them to get people talking, to help us get to know our students and to foster transformations. The heart of *Your Future Now* is contained in these 17 Questions.

We quickly and affectionately turned Cal's name into a verb. We began to say, "I Cal Crowed him/her" when we took the time to have meaningful conversations that focused on achievements, unexplored potentials, strengths and opportunities. In Appreciative Inquiry, the question *is* the intervention. As the interviewee considers each question, a positive core forms from which untapped potential can arise. Students evolve before our eyes as they frame their reality in new ways. Using them sidesteps the need for staff to problem-solve; rather, the questions encourage students to become aware of their already existing successes. From that platform of recognized accomplishments, they see their own capacity to problem-solve for themselves.

> *Asking a question can change our reality and that of others.**

The 17 Questions are based on three assumptions:

1. Everyone wants to feel competent, confident and connected.
2. Everyone wants to be and feel successful, to have a voice, to contribute and to make a difference.
3. Everyone needs someone to listen and to care.

Appreciative Inquiry is part of the positive psychology movement that has taken hold in many parts of the country. It is a way of posing provocative questions that require individuals to think differently about "the way we do things here" (culture). It introduces dynamism, self-agency, and positivity. Most of the 17 Questions we use at Scriber cause power to shift from "I can't" to "What if I could?"

Appreciative Inquiry techniques, originally developed by David L. Cooperrider and associates at Case Western University, are used widely in organizations to search for the best in people and to consider what a system might look like when it is most alive and effective. As conversations shift from problem-focused to a focus on successes and dreams, entire organizational cultures transform.

Cal applied these concepts as he thought about schools. Early in our work, he asked, "How much of student learning is cognitive, how much is emotional and how much is meaning-making? Where are students most alive? If we want more students to succeed in high school and continue their education, on which of these three areas should we concentrate?"

These questions also seek to curtail the occurrence of students who say, "I went through school and nobody knew me." Below, we have collected conversations using these questions.

---

*Quotes in this chapter are general principles of the Appreciative Inquiry philosophy.

The 17 Questions

1. Please say more about that. (encourages talk)
2. That sounds interesting. Could you elaborate a bit more? (encourages talk)
3. How would you feel if...? (you could do math, you could make it work, you did like school?) (shifts conversation from a negative position of weakness to a position of strength and possibilities)
4. What would it mean to you or How would your life be different if...(you could do math, you could make it work, you did like school?) (shifts conversation from a negative position of weakness to a position of strength and possibilities)
5. What would you think about...? (getting some extra help, trying a new approach, moving away from the "friends" who don't seem to be helping you?) (focuses on change, taking action, agency)
6. What would it mean if everyone in this class could create a successful future? What suggestions do you have for making this occur? (youth gives voice; makes contribution; has future orientation) (focuses on change, taking action, agency)
7. What does it mean for you to/when...? (addresses values)
8. It sounds like...is pretty important to you. (addresses values)
9. On the one hand, you...and on the other hand, you... (addresses ambivalence)
10. How did you decide (to, that)...? (addresses decision making)
11. How would you describe what was going on there? (elicits person's view of reality)
12. How did you learn to do that? (focuses on skills and learning and passion)
13. How did you develop an interest in that? (focuses on skills and learning and passion)
14. What is there about...that you find appealing? (focuses on skills and learning and passion)
15. What would it take to change that? (Used when students talk about reasons they "can't" do something, or something won't work)
16. I keep hearing a theme/message that... (lets students know that we are listening and analyzing)
17. A little while ago I thought I heard you say...then a little later I thought I heard you say..., and now I'm hearing... How do we put all of this together? What do you think is going on? (lets students know that we are listening and analyzing)

Theme: ENCOURAGE TALK

1. *Please say more about that.*
2. *That sounds interesting. Could you elaborate a bit more?*

[handwritten: allows you to keep the ball in the students' court.]

Peter Folta, Social Studies

I am still working on this student—it's not going to be easy with him. He is showing up and smiling a lot more, but he is still shy about turning in work and contributing to class discussions. This behavior is a departure from what he demonstrated before I showed interest in him; before, he was constantly on his phone—head down, eyes down, trying to not be seen.

Before, I probably would have challenged this student and lost him early on. But this year I got to know him, and that may have made all the difference.

"Please say more about that," was what I said to him when I called him out to talk in the hallway.

No one in his family had graduated from high school, he told me. Not his dad, not his mom, not his brother. His brother had preceded him at another high school, and when he showed up years later in Mr. J's class, he was told, "You will never pass my class. I had your brother."

That name—he remembered that teacher's name. It stained his face when he said it.

I knew right then I had more to learn from him than maybe he could learn from me. Just in that one moment. He would never forget that name and I would never forget that expression on his face.

Marjie Bowker, English

The other day B showed up to class and sat in the back of the room, hunched over, looking at his phone. He had only 20% for his grade and had been showing up randomly all quarter–even after begging me to let him into my full class. I knew this student well; he was one of my favorites, despite the fact that the first statement he usually made when he sat down was, "I don't want to be here."

After the rest of the class got started on writing poetry, I sat down next to him. Even though we had a good relationship, he shot me a look that warned me "not to start" with him. Which, I must admit, is still my instinct–to mention students' poor attendance and grades. But, fortunately, I can now recognize that tendency and redirect it.

"How are things going, B?" I asked, and I saw his face relax a little.

"Oh, OK. How are you?" he returned.

We talked a little about his job, which he had just lost, and about his living situation, which was not good–and had not been good–for years. Then I noticed what seemed to be a new tattoo on his forearm. It was beautifully detailed, so I commented on that and asked why he chose that particular picture (**say more about that…**)

"I wanted to have something to remember my grandpa."

I asked him about his grandpa (**say more about that…**). After he talked for a while, I said, **"It sounds like your relationship with your grandpa was really important to you."**

He began to tell me about all of the special things they used to do together. In a short time, he was asking about the poem the class was engaged in writing, even though he had no chance of passing the class. This led to a discussion about his life, his goal to work on cars, where he was at with credits. I told him to come to my computer so I could look up that information.

After seeing that he had earned only eight credits as a junior (out of 22 to graduate), I asked him, **"On a scale of one to ten, how important is earning a diploma?"** I've become accustomed to asking this question to determine where the rest of the discussion should go–whether someone in his situation might be better off getting a GED, or at least considering other options. This way I can make sure we are on the same page.

"About a seven," he answered. "Actually, it's a ten to my family, a five to me." This led to more conversation about family (**say more about that**) until B finally said, "Marjie, why are you being all inquisitive with me today?"

"Well, because I care about you," I said.

He just shrugged and continued talking about his plan for his life. I asked him **what it would take to move the seven to an eight,** and we began to discuss his difficulty with math and his desire to be on his own.

Regardless of what happens, I was truly interested in his story about his grandfather. I know if I would have said anything about the assignment first, it would have been a meaningless transaction to him—and for me, too. My assignments are only meaningful if he sees the connection, and the connection was what I was establishing in that interaction. My approach has changed; I now look for the underlying cause of the behavior before addressing anything else.

Liza Behrendt, Leadership and Entry

Today I talked with a student about a conflict in which someone was reportedly creating drama about a situation for which we did not have all of the facts. She was reacting to this student's talk, yet shared that she wanted desperately to find a way to transcend the pettiness which was arising.

I asked her to "**say more about that,**" so many times, and every time it yielded discoveries for her. In the end, after many mini-discoveries, she recognized that she could continue to focus on the positive and have compassion for the other student. She thought she could at least remain neutral, or maybe even try to help the student check out what had actually happened in order to gain more solid facts regarding what needed to be done.

She also expressed the wish to learn other ways to cope and get along with others. It was clear to me that she was growing inside and learning how to manage her own reactions and responses, which is a great skill for her future.

Leighanne Law, Library and English

A girl in entry was having a difficult time with her "Who Am I?" project (she was supposed to present parts of herself and her past to the rest of the class). They were asked to identify many things about themselves, and she was stuck. By asking her to **"say more about that,"** she elaborated a lot and I found out so many things about her. After that she was able to do her project with ease.

Dave Zwaschka, English

I use this question the most; in fact, in the first part of the year as I struggled to know exactly which ones to ask, it was my "go-to" response for just about every situation. The desire to be understood is the highest human need, and asking someone to "say more" fosters an inquisitiveness that is rare in our culture. Often we jump to giving advice, but inviting students to expand gets to the heart of the issue by probing just a bit more.

> *Whatever we focus on increases and becomes our reality.*

Even now that I'm more comfortable using some of the other questions, this is still a great one because it fits both personal and academic conversations. As we compose our personal narratives this week, I invite students to **"please say more about"** all kinds of things. Yesterday we generated physical details about a character in a photograph. As we did, one student said, "He smells like an old sailor." When I asked him to **please say more about** what an old sailor might smell like, he thought for a moment and then provided details ("He smells briny; I catch a whiff of cod, timber, stale beer and Old Spice") of such precision that the rest of the class nodded in unison.

(handwritten: Goes beyond just giving advice. Kids actually imagine themselves being successful.)

Theme: SHIFT FROM NEGATIVE POSITION OF WEAKNESS TO A POSITION OF STRENGTH AND POSSIBILITIES

3. *How would you feel if...? (you could do math, you could make it work, you did like school, you passed all of your classes, you did make it to school/class on time)*
4. *What would it mean to you or How would your life be different if... ? (you could do math, you could make it work, you did like school, you passed all of your classes, you did make it to school/class on time)*

Zachary Taylor, College and Career Specialist

If a student tells me "School sucks!" my response is to ask **"What if it didn't suck?"** or **"What if I could put you in a situation that wouldn't suck?"** or **"What's your plan?"**

Instead of putting students on the defensive about their current stance on school, our job at Scriber is to shift their focus to the future. I don't just give a student a packet of information on postsecondary education or jobs, we try to take the next step and have students fill out scholarship applications, apply for jobs, or send out requests for additional information about a college while in my office.

The day one student graduated from high school, I immediately drove her over to the local community college, had her register with the college and then set her up with Services for Students with Disabilities (SSD).

Marjie Bowker, English

We were reading *Enrique's Journey* in English 10 and most of the class was engaged with it. But one student was not. He put his head down and didn't do any of the writing assignments.

One day I asked him to come out in the hall to talk while the rest of the class worked. (The quarter had just started, so I didn't know him well yet.)

"Tell me a little about yourself," I said.

"What do you want to know?"

"Well, I'm wondering why your head is down a lot."

"What you need to know is that I don't like school."

"Say more about that."

"Well, I'm only here to stay out of jail. I just want to go to community college so I can do something I'm interested in."

"What's that?"

"I want to work on cars."

"What do you like about working on cars?"

"I have to do something hands-on. I can't just sit there. I get so bored."

"That's good to know. Will you be content working for someone else, or do you think you might want to own a shop someday?"

"Yes, sure. I want to own a shop."

"Would it make a difference to know that earning a diploma would help you to do that?"

He paused, then said, "Hey, don't take it personally. You're a really good teacher. I just don't like school."

"What if you did like it? How would that change things?"

"That would be nice," he repeated. "But I'm just putting in time, so it doesn't matter. Don't worry about me."

"I'm not worried about you, but I do care that what we're doing is meaningful to you while you're here. Because we're talking a lot of hours to just 'put in time.'"

"Yeah, I guess. I'm just really tired today."

"What would you think about meeting with Zach (Career Specialist) to talk about some of this?"

"Maybe."

"OK, I just want you to know that I like you and I think you're really smart. I would like to help you to find meaning in school."

He smiled. "I appreciate that. Thank you."

He came back to class and didn't put his head down. He didn't open the book, but he did listen and respond to a few of the events that occurred. Mostly, I was grateful that we had this conversation.

Two weeks later:

His head has not been down nearly as much. We have been talking about the Dream Act and are reading both "pro" and "con" articles regarding this issue.

When we read the "con" side, he gets really animated as he offers his opinions—so much so that another girl in class says (to the whole class), "In the five years I have known him, I have never seen him care about anything like this in school."

He kind of laughs and says, "Well, it's just that this issue isn't easy. I can see both sides.

Later, as we read, he is listening intently, commenting often. It's progress.

During one student's parent conference we were discussing how he stayed up really late, got up late and how he was always tired at school, even though he had a late start.

I asked him, **"How would things be different if you were getting more sleep and were more awake in your classes?"**

I was surprised at how quickly he answered this question and how much he had to say about it. "I would feel better, like I'm getting things done," he said. "It would feel good, instead of sloughing off, you know?"

Then his mom added, "And you would be getting more stickers on your chart." (His Road to Success poster that shows all 88 quarter credits needed—Chapter Nine.)

"Yeah," he said, and smiled.

He left the meeting feeling positive about his potential to start getting things done. A few months later, I awarded him the "Most Transformed" Award at our recognition assembly for how far he had come in such a short time.

Another student was in a similar situation. With hardly any credits, he often overslept, skipped classes, and took a lot of time to "work things out" with his girlfriend during class time. He blamed a lot of people for his situation.

"How would your life be different if you took responsibility for making a decision about school?" I asked.

He also answered quickly. "It would be really different. If I took responsibility, then I would go to bed earlier and wake up more ready to be here and to get things done. I would know that it is my choice and that no one was telling me what to do."

He left our meeting feeling empowered—at least for that one moment. He did not turn things around like the other did; however, placing things in his court took the responsibility off of me and placed it onto him. I think he was used to getting lectured and that he appreciated being treated as an adult.

Barb Kathol, Attendance

As I become aware of patterns with students who are continually late, I find myself starting conversations with them, asking questions such as, "Why did you choose Scriber? Why are you late? How do you get to school each day? Do you have friends that attend here? Do you like the classes that were assigned? Which class is your favorite?"

> *The only way to understand another person is through questioning and listening.*

The answers are often, "I don't know anyone here. I travel so far, I take three buses. I missed my connecting bus. I don't like school. My ride was late."

Then I ask, **"How would you feel if you made it to class on time?** Let's map out your route and your morning time schedule.

This makes students very happy. They often respond by asking, "You'll do that for me?"

Many students can't believe that I would take the time to listen to them and to help problem solve.

Another student shares that he doesn't know anyone. "My other school was so big, no one cared about what I did, so neither did I."

I ask, **"How could you** meet other students here? Do you want to get involved in some school activities? **How would you like to be** part of a group of students that take clothing and blankets to the homeless?"

"Yes," he answers quietly, and his journey into the Scriber family begins.

Each day now he stops by to say "hello" and is surprised I remember his name. He attends regularly and is so proud of himself.

"What will help you to be on time to school? How can I help you?" I ask another student who is continually late.

"It's not my fault," she says. "My friend is always late picking me up."

"**How could you change that?** Let me look up your address and find the bus route.

Now the student rides the bus. I don't see her in the mornings anymore because she is on time, but she does stop by daily to say hi and often thanks me for caring.

Coley Armstrong, Entry and Social Studies

I recently spoke with a student about **how it would feel** if he could pass Entry and be successful as a full-time Scriber student. He reported that he did not like having to be in either the Entry or the STEP program and would like to have a normal schedule again. I asked him again **how he would feel if** he passed Entry and was granted that schedule. He reported that his attitude would improve and he could see himself graduating high school.

Greg Lange, Student Transition Education Program (STEP)

I have taken great delight in asking students two questions:

"**It seems that**... (not knowing, missing school, skipping my class) **is very important to you. Could you tell me more about that?**"

After a student tells me that he/she doesn't know about xyz, I ask, "**If you** could **know, how would that feel?**"

Students are usually savvy enough to recognize that it is no longer *my* issue to deal with and places them squarely in the sights of self-responsibility. It has been a pleasure to also watch other students witness these interactions. I believe that the message received by those questioned has made a positive impact on those observing.

Theme: FOCUS ON CHANGE, TAKING ACTION, AGENCY

5. *What would you think about . . .? (getting some extra help, trying a new approach, moving away from the "friends" who don't seem to be helping you?) (focuses on change, taking action, agency)*
6. *What would it mean if everyone in this class could create a successful future? What suggestions do you have for making this occur? (youth gives voice, makes contribution, has future orientation)*

Trinity Meriwood, Business Education and Graphic Arts

I had a student in Computer Applications class who really struggled. He would often open up Microsoft Paint and doodle some highly artistic pieces, which wasn't doing anything for his credit in Computer Applications. But then something dawned on me. I asked him, "**What would you think about being in my Graphic Arts class?** You seem to really like drawing within the computer environment. The software we use is even better than MS Paint."

He's very shy; he hasn't said more than ten words in an entire term. But he looked at me with a slight smile and answered, "Yeah. Ok." This interaction doesn't seem very significant, but it's what's happening in my current graphic arts class that demonstrates the change in him. Now he actually seeks help and asks how to do things in the software.

He's a student that went from zero success to a high amount of success in a class that actually interested him.

Marjie Bowker, English

One of my students had been very set on becoming a firefighter, but at his last conference told me, "I don't want to do that anymore. I heard it's impossible to get in."

I asked him, "**What would you think about setting goals in steps rather than having that one huge goal?** Something you could accomplish first without having to kill your dream altogether?"

"Well, that would make some sense," he answered. "I could see doing that."

We got on the WOIS (career information) system and looked at jobs that were similar to firefighting. And just like that, he was back on track.

Theme: ADDRESS VALUES

7. *What does it mean for you to/when...?*
8. *It sounds like..is pretty important to you.*

Marjie Bowker, English

I felt really annoyed when this student walked into Silent Reading wearing his black hoodie sweatshirt with a picture of a big-breasted woman in a tiny bikini. We had talked about the inappropriate nature of the sweatshirt for school attire the previous week.

I asked him to turn it inside out, but he refused and looked at me sideways as he walked out the door at the end of class. I said, "You know that the administration is going to side with me on this."

His face darkened into a snarl. "Marjie, why are you making such a big deal about this?"

I have a good relationship with this student. I have him in class in addition to Family; in English, he is usually the first to see a connection in literature. He got into a lot of trouble in middle school, but he is having a positive experience so far at Scriber and the sweatshirt dilemma is our first negative interaction of the year. I knew what he needed was a conversation—rather than a threat—from me.

When I got the chance, I called him out of his next class. "I don't want us to leave things like this," I said. First, I asked him to tell me a funny story from the day and then I told him one, too. When the tension was broken, I said, **"It seems that this sweatshirt is very important to you."**

He told me that he spent his Christmas money on it. That it was really warm and comfortable, and that others responded to that picture better than the pictures on his other sweatshirts.

"What message does that picture send?" I asked, and he went back to the cost of the sweatshirt and that his friends thought it was cool.

I asked if I could share what message his sweatshirt was sending to me and he agreed. I told him it seemed that the girl's breasts were the most important part of her, especially since most of her face was cut off. "Is that the message you want to send to others?" I asked.

"No," he answered.

"Say more about that."

He told me he felt the sexes should be equal, and that he had stood up for girls in many situations.

"It sounds like protecting people is important to you," I said. He agreed and then told a specific story about a time he stood up for a girl over an issue involving discrimination.

Eventually he said, "OK, Marjie. I get it. I respect what you are saying. I won't wear it to school anymore." Then he added, "But I will still wear it at home."

"Got it," I said. "Was this conversation OK for you?" I've become better at this part lately— requesting some kind of reflection on my conversations with students.

At first he seemed confused by the question and repeated that he would still wear the sweatshirt at home.

"No, I mean, did this conversation help?" I clarified.

"Oh, yeah!" he answered. "Actually, I appreciate it that you explained it to me. Because I really didn't understand what the big deal was. But now I get it."

I said, "I want you to know that I respect how you treat others and I think you are a very smart, thoughtful person. In English you are one of my most insightful students." After a pause I asked, **"How does it feel** to hear me say that?"

Again, he deflected a bit and said he would still wear the sweatshirt at home. After all, he had paid $40 for it.

"OK, forget the sweatshirt," I said. "The sweatshirt doesn't matter to me at all right now. What matters is how you feel about what I said about you. That you are a smart, thoughtful person who treats people with respect."

Then he smiled. "Oh, well, that feels really good, actually. It's nice to know you think that."

"Good. Are we good then?" I held out my hand and we shook.

Part Two:

I know this will shock other high school teachers, but it wasn't all unicorns and rainbows after this great discussion. He did wear the sweatshirt again. I found out he was taking it off or turning it inside out before coming into my class for a few weeks, then forgot to do that one day.

As soon as he walked in and realized I saw it, he groaned and hit his forehead for his mistake.

I called an administrator to talk to him at that point, but it was not a power struggle at all; in fact, we were both laughing about it. He knew it would be my next step. As he left to face his sweatshirt's final doom, he said, "I meant no disrespect to you, Marjie. It's just a really comfortable sweatshirt."

"No disrespect felt," I answered, and I meant it.

Enforcing rules by just stating them rarely helps. It's the conversation behind the rules that matters, and if approached in the right way—even after approaching it the wrong way—there is a chance for negative transaction to be replaced with a positive transformation based on relationship. Things are rarely seamless when it comes to teenagers, but it sure helps to have the tools to go to a place of non-confrontation with them.

> **Theme: ADDRESS AMBIVALENCE**
>
> 9.   *On the one hand, you...and on the other hand, you...*

Leighanne Law, Library and English

A student of mine, K, who at various points during the year has had an "A" as well as a "No Credit" in my English class, was staying after school for a program called "Thrive City" led by Sarah Philley. This program encourages kids to become leaders as they reflect on failures and successes, from hitting rock bottom to learning to ask for help, to—finally—thriving.

She came into the library with another student to analyze an article about Steve Jobs' early experiences with failure.

"Leighanne," she asked, "can you help me think of a time when I failed at something and saw the experience in a negative light?"

"Well, what comes to mind for you?" I asked. We bantered back and forth about a few ideas and some old childhood hurts, but no examples that held enough weight for her.

"What about last quarter? Do you think you could write about what happened last quarter?"

"Oh. I guess. Like how?" she asked.

"Take me through the big picture of last quarter. How was it in the beginning and then **how did it change?**"

"I was a really good student in the beginning of the quarter and then I just stopped caring. I skipped class a lot, wouldn't do work. You know. But I never thought about myself negatively, you know? I could still see how I would pull through it all."

"What changed for you? **What made you decide to stop trying in class?**" She told me that some of the choices she was making outside of school were still currently affecting her in school and were "making her a bad student."

"So," I said, **"I heard you say earlier that you didn't view that experience or yourself negatively, and now I hear you categorize yourself as a "bad" student. Can you tell me more about that?"**

She paused. And thought. And frowned. And said, "Oh. Huh." and paused again. "I guess I did. Hmmm. I'm going to need to think about that some more."

We left the conversation at that, but the next day she came to class, got really invested in the reading and had quite a lot to say. I don't know if that was a transformation, but it sure felt like it.

Part Two:

A week after I wrote the above, she skipped my class. She had rescheduled her parent-teacher conference, but forgot to let her stepdad know. He was at school when she returned with her friend and he was aggravated when he discovered she had skipped.

Later that day, she returned to the library for the "Thrive City" after-school program and wished me a happy birthday. I once might have talked to her about the consequences of skipping class. Instead, I decided to ask her some questions.

"What happened today?" I asked, and she began to tell me about a struggle she had been going through with her stepdad.

"Really? **Can you say more about that?**"

She explained more about the disconnect she was feeling.

"**It sounds like building relationships are really important to you...**"

This statement opened the conversation dramatically and she was candid about how she is terrified of being alone. So afraid, in fact, that this fear is driving her to make dangerous decisions for herself. She acknowledges that she sees the dangers and understands the consequences, but makes–in her words, "bad" choices anyway because it is far worse to be alone or abandoned. "Also," she said, "I really enjoy what I've been doing."

As she spoke, I wrote down what she said. Then, I read to her what I had written.

"**What I've been hearing you talk about recently...it sounds like you're moving away from your comfort zone...the identity that you once were, the way you once saw yourself. Can you say some more about that?**"

"Yeah, I really am. That's it. The way I used to be is so boring and lonely and sheltered. So now I make myself available to people all the time. Like, I don't really make the time to do school work if people want to hang out. The way I used to be was so different." She told me that she is now hungry for new experiences, fun, and being around people all the time.

"**What would it be like for you if you could find some of those things at school? How would things change for you?**"

"I would probably want to be in school more."

"What would make you want to come to *English* more often?"

"Well, you know, I'm not really into the science fiction-writing thing."

"Yeah, I noticed it didn't seem very engaging to you."

"I really feel like writing this kind of stuff, lately. Like poetry. Something serious. I feel like I'm scraping away at my issues, which sounds like a bad thing, right? Like I'm hurting myself. But my issues are like hard stone and I have to keep digging at them."

> *We see what our imaginative horizon allows us to see.*

"**What would you think about** writing a personal narrative, like what Marjie's class does (see Chapter Eleven)? A way for you to "scrape" at these ideas and maybe work through them?"

Her eyes lit up as a grin slid across her face.

"I would LOVE that. I would love to do that."

"Awesome. Let's work together to do that, we'll do some work shopping and brainstorming. You can even write another narrative in place of the last fiction story, if you'd like. Do you want me to get some things ready for class tomorrow so we can jump right in?"

"Yes, please!"

At that moment she was called into another room, but a few minutes later she came back and said, "I have to tell you, Leighanne, how much it means to me that we had this talk. That I skipped your class—on your *birthday*—and that you still care enough about me to ask how you can make class more interesting for me. That means so much to me."

Since that conversation, she has been a writing fiend. She has been exploring this idea of how love and fear have been affecting her life lately. I told her how proud I was of her deep reflection and growth and that I would like to include our conversations in this book. **I asked her how that would make her feel.**

"I'd be totally ok with that! Oh, I need to tell you something. Today, two of my friends were thinking about skipping 5th period and normally, I would have gone with them. But I decided not to skip because I wanted to come here and do this work." And with a look that told me, "Excuse me, please, but I really must get back to work," she once again began to "scrape" away at her personal narrative.

> **Theme: ADDRESS DECISION-MAKING**
>
> 10. *How did you decide (to, that)...?*

Tammy Stapleton, STEP Program

One student told me he could not do algebra problems. He didn't understand why he needed to learn it; he knew he couldn't do it anyway. When **I asked him if he had ever thought about what it would be like if he could do algebra,** he replied negatively. Then I asked **how he decided he couldn't do algebra.** I then got out the work packet and starting going through some of the problems with him. He was surprised to discover that he actually *could* do algebra.

He and his brother are now working on their seventh algebra packet. Each morning we work on problems together. He realized that quadratic equations are not that bad if you learn to do them one step at a time.

Marjie Bowker, English

This student had a really rocky past; he came to us with hardly any credits and has struggled to stay in class or complete anything. He is very private about what has happened in his life, but is always respectful to his teachers while refusing to do work.

When asked about his interests or goals for the future he would usually say something about his interest in nature, but could never pinpoint where he wanted to go with that.

Therefore, I was very surprised one day when I revisited this topic. "Have you given any more thought about what kind of future you want?"

He lit up. "Yes."

I was surprised at his enthusiasm. "What are you thinking?"

"I want to be a teacher."

"Wow! How did you decide that?"

"Well, I've always connected with teachers," he said, "and I feel like I could connect with students. And I think junior high is a really important time, when people begin to make important decisions."

"Yes, you do connect. That's right. I can see it, I really can! What subject do you want to teach?"

"Junior high science."

"Interesting. **What made you choose** that?"

"That's the only class I ever passed in middle school."

"But not now. Look at all of the classes you're passing..." (we were looking at his grades and his Road to Success poster at the time, see Chapter Nine).

"Yeah."

"How does it feel to be doing so well and to know what you want to do?"

"It feels really good."

He left with the biggest smile on his face that day. I feel like I saw a transformation take place right before my eyes.

> **Theme: ELICIT PERSON'S VIEW OF REALITY**
>
> 11. *How would you describe what was going on there?*

Kanoe Vierra, Dean of Students and English

Every year, a number of business professionals and college representatives give presentations about programs and jobs at our Futures Fair. All the morning sessions had gone well and many of our students were engaged and asking good questions.

However, during the afternoon session, I was called out of a meeting and was told, "There's a new Entry student in the office who is very upset and asked specifically to speak with you."

I knew it was important if they were interrupting me. I asked the student, who was extremely agitated, to come in to my office so that we could have a chat.

I asked her, "**How would you describe what happened during the presentation?**"

She described herself as someone who asked lots of questions and, apparently, someone in the session didn't like that. This person had told her to "shut up," and she had responded in "not so kind and pretty ways" and things had escalated in both volume and words. After all, she was very curious about the topic.

I asked her, "What was being presented?"

"Nursing," she responded.

I followed up with, "Really? **Tell me more.**"

She went on to tell me about her family's experience in this field and about her interest in pursuing it. She also told me that her other career interest was in diesel mechanics.

"That's really interesting," I said. "Two opposite types of careers choices. **How did you decide** that a diesel mechanic would be a possible career choice for you?"

"I've always been interested in cars and trucks and I have experience working on engines, both gasoline and diesel, and I've enjoyed making them run again," she said. "In a way it is much like nursing except that one is alive and the other is mechanical."

After a while, she said. "Thank you, Kanoe, you have helped me to calm down and to really focus again on what is important. I want to finish my high school education, then move on to my career of choice."

For this student, refocusing on her future goals was a positive way for her to calm down and actually enjoy the rest of the presentation.

Theme: FOCUS ON SKILLS, LEARNING AND PASSION

    12. *How did you learn to do that?*

    13. *How did you develop an interest in that?*

    14. *What is there about...that you find appealing?*

Liza Behrendt, Entry

During a session in which Cal guided me as I interviewed a student, we touched on several of the questions that focus on skills, learning and passion. I began by asking her what she had in mind for a career.

"I want to be a special needs teacher or I want to be a little kids' teacher, kindergarten through 3rd grade. I want to go to Western to learn about it first."

"And **how did you decide both of those things?**"

"I went to the college fair and met the people from Western, they came over to talk to us about it, and it seemed like the best school. I want to go there because it's not huge, but it's not really small either. So, it's an ok size. And the teachers really care about students' success."

It seemed that she was echoing the aims of *Your Future Now*.

She continued, "And the reason why I wanted to be a teacher is because I've always worked really well with little kids with special needs. My aunt is a special ed teacher and a lot of my relatives have special needs, so I'd like to work with them."

"**Could you say more about** your family?" Cal asked. She described several situations that relations of hers were dealing with in the realm of special needs.

"I think that special needs kids are pretty much the same; people just treat them differently."

"So if you were a special needs teacher, what would you be doing about that?" Cal asked.

"Treat them the same. I would just...it's like if you were teaching a regular class, but have more attention on them."

I wanted to honor this already-forming skill in the Appreciative Inquiry style. "**It sounds like you have an**

ability that not everybody has, to see the intelligence of people who might have some special needs yet still have so much to offer. Does that sound right?"

"Yeah." (Smile.)

Dave Zwaschka, English

Prior to reading an article explaining the Dream Act and its goal of providing education and eventual citizenship to children of undocumented immigrants, I asked students to write responses to the following questions on sticky notes:

What is one dream you **have for your future?**

What career interests you the most? What kind of job do you most want to pursue?

If you're interested in further education after high school, what would you like to study?

What kind of family would you like to have? Would you like to be single or get married, and/or have children?

Students then took their sticky notes to the corresponding poster around the classroom. As the posters filled up, I asked them to stand next to the response they felt most strongly about. These were interesting in their variety, and so were students' insights when probed. During a full-class discussion, I used several of the 17 Questions.

One student mentioned a desire to become a fireman or paramedic. I asked, "**How did you decide** to pursue this career?"

He answered, "Ever since I can remember, I've hated to see suffering. I accidentally caused the death of a squirrel when I was little and it almost killed me thinking about it. I still think about it now. I want to be someone who keeps people from being hurt, who can save people who are suffering. This has always been a strong motivation in my life."

Another student's dream was to become self-actualized, to develop his inner self. When I asked him, "**Please say more about that,**" he said, "The biggest challenge in life is the work we do inside ourselves, the way we form our own personalities to handle life's challenges."

I was interested in his response, so **I asked him to elaborate** on his thoughts about self-actualization after class. I began by asking "**How did you develop an interest in this?**"

He said, "I started working on myself about a year and a half ago. At that time, I was suffering from depression and a lot of anxiety. I had trouble holding a conversation with anybody. I decided to set a goal to become a little better every day. I began listening to meditation tapes and reading books about how to meditate. I've worked at this a lot, about being happy where I am.

> *We want to create a reality that works for everyone.*

"**What has it meant for you to have chosen this as a goal?**" I asked.

He said, "The past year and a half has been the best time of my life. Life-changing, really. I now have some life goals. I can now see my future ahead of me."

In response to the question "Do you want to go to college, and if so, what would you study?" one student answered, "I want to know everything, I want to study everything. Life-long learning? That's what I want."

He was hesitant to name a major he might study at this point, though he did say, "I want to study history and ethics. They're connected."

When asked "What kind of family would you like to have?" one student said, "I want to marry a Latina because all I have to do is work and put food on the table and she would clean the house and take care of my son and daughter." When I probed deeper with "**What is there about having children that you find appealing?**" he noted, "Family is the most important thing—nothing else comes close. I want to have two children: A son first, and then a daughter. That way, my son can watch over his little sister and protect her from harm."

This full-class conversation, which lasted perhaps 20 minutes, afforded us all the chance to go deeper than the initial sticky-note responses. Students enjoyed sharing personal attitudes and aspirations, and the class culture seemed strengthened by honest and heartfelt exchange. Students listened respectfully to each other, considering other's personal stories and then sharing their own.

Peter Folta, Social Studies

The first time I had this student in class, he fell asleep nearly every day he attended.

The second time he was in my class, he was like a new man. I discovered what a thoughtful and intelligent student he was, and I was impressed.

One day I asked him, "**How did you learn to make such a change in your life**, you know, in terms of being a student?"

He smiled and leaned back in his chair. "I have narcolepsy, but I outgrew it."

"You outgrew it, **how did you do that?**"

"I kind of made up mind that it wasn't going to affect me. I started exercising. I saw that I was on the wrong path, and that I needed to graduate."

Marjie Bowker, English

The other day I was working with a student on her personal narrative and noticed a very skilled drawing on her notebook. I asked her if she had done it and she answered, "Yes."

Instead of saying, "That's so good!" I asked her, "**How did you learn to do that?**"

With this one simple question, I learned that at the age of two her mother had asked her to draw a bunny and she had done it straight out of her head. She had known what it was and how to draw it without any help. She said she had just "always" known how to draw. We talked about natural talent and what a gift it was. After a bit, we went back to the writing, but it was a great moment, full of meaning.

Theme: REALIZATION OF STRENGTHS AND CAPABILITIES

15. What would it take to change that? (Used when students talk about reasons they "can't" do something, or something won't work)
    Often, it's helpful to begin with this question: On a scale of one to ten, how important is…(getting a diploma)?

    And then some follow-ups:
    On a scale of one to ten, what is your confidence level to accomplish this?
    What would it take to move that 7 to an 8?
    What would it take to make those two numbers match?

Andrea Hillman, Associate Principal

The 17 Questions guide the difficult conversations we have during conferences with parents and students. Just last week I was in a meeting with a parent, a teacher, a counselor and a student who is struggling with attendance.

Through focusing on his desires to get an education, a diploma and a career in the long term, he was asked, "**On a scale of one to ten, how determined are you to get a high-school diploma?**"

He responded, "10."

Next question, "**On a scale of one to ten, how would you rate the effort you're putting into it?**"

Then it got real. "Um, probably a 4."

The room became quiet, and in that silence, he connected that his own decisions, his own effort, was impacting his plan for the future. But he wasn't let off the hook. The next question was, "**What would it take for the effort you put in to match your determination to get a diploma?**" and the conversation continued along these lines.

This is not an isolated incident at this school. Teachers, counselors and other staff members are always able to refocus the conversation on plans for the future and how to reach their goals.

Peter Folta, Social Studies

A student was doing make-up work in my class one afternoon. I hadn't seen her for days, so I asked her, "Could I talk to you for a little while?"

"Okaaayyy..." she answered.

"I have missed you in class recently. Has school been your number one priority lately?"

"Well, I would say graduating in June is."

"And how is that going?"

"I don't know, I am a little nervous."

"Well, **what would it mean if high school (being here now), were your number one priority?**"

"I would probably show up more, other things just come first, but I would be caught up.

"And, **what would it take to change that**, to make attending school your number one priority?"

"I don't know. I want to be here, I mean like after my six-day weekend, I wanted to be here a lot more. I have been dealing with some sucky things. And there is transportation, the bus schedules don't match up with my schedule."

"What about you, **is there anything you can control** about this?"

"I don't know, getting more control of my clock, my time. I am not sure."

"**I keep hearing a theme that** you have a lot of 'things' going on?"

"Yeah, I am really nervous about college next year."

"**What would it take to change that?**"

"More assurance about college. No one in my family knows anything; no one has gone to college. I have looked up stuff on college. Someone said that if you have fun in high school, you can't have fun in college."

"I don't know about that. I think if you study what you want to study, it can be fun."

"Well, I want to study hospitality, being a stewardess, you know. But some people don't think I could do it, because they say I am a bitch."

"I would never say that about you. You are very friendly," I said, "Maybe a little flighty, but not mean."

"That's cool!" she said with a big smile.

"We need to get you more information about college. Have you talked to Zach (our college and career specialist)?"

Marjie Bowker, English

I have watched this student evolve in tremendous ways over the last three years. She came to us a very angry person and would often blow up at the tiniest things. But lately she is soft and quiet. She is bright, a really good writer, and has gained a ton of confidence. But she just can't seem to make it to school regularly. She has battled her mother for a very long time.

After she told me about the latest incident, I asked her, "**On a scale of one to ten, how important is it to you to earn your diploma?**"

"Ten," she answered quickly.

"**And on a scale of one to ten, how much confidence do you have in yourself to achieve this goal?**"

"Um, about a 6."

"**How can we move that number up?**"

"Probably by accomplishing some small things, like being here consistently."

"OK, that sounds good to me. On another scale of one to ten, **how much do you want to be free?**"

"Eleven," she said.

"**So how would you describe what is going on between you and your mother?**"

This question elicited more stories about their dysfunctional relationship. "She will never let me leave," she says.

"How old are you?" I asked.

"Almost 21."

"**How would your life be different if you made your own rules?**"

"I don't know."

"Try to answer."

"Better?"

"What could you do to change that, to take control for yourself?"

"Well, I could start by graduating."

"That would be a very good, solid first step," I said. "I know it's a "ten" for you when it comes to importance, but if you don't make it here consistently, your actions are at what number on that scale?"

"Probably under five."

"So matching up your actions with your desires would be pretty important to you? So that you can get yourself free?"

"Yeah."

I saw some lights go on during this conversation; maybe some ideas will take hold and grow. There is hope.

Brenna Hanson, Registrar and Counseling Secretary

Based on previous conversations with this student, I knew that she had some friendship issues that she was trying to move past. When the issues first started, I asked her a few questions: **What do you think you need to do to move forward?** and **Where do you see yourself when everything has settled?**

Initially, an explanation of how sad and mad this situation had made her was her only response; everything else was held in. As time passed, I would occasionally bring up the same two questions and slowly she began to open up. I feel as though the process of saying things out loud and talking them out with someone was helping her gain a clearer understanding; I saw the light flicker on and she began to accept the outcome of what had happened.

Now she realizes that these friendships were holding her back. She expresses a desire to surround herself with motivated people, to graduate from high school, find a good job and be more adventurous. She is happy about where she is going and what is in her future.

Overall, I felt these conversations were successful. It was a good reflection for her and exciting for me to witness her process. She went from feeling very lost and confused to developing a sense of self-worth.

Most importantly, she came to all of her conclusions by herself. While I was asking questions here and there, she was able to develop a method of problem-solving that worked best for her. Self-reflection and turning the conversation back on the student helps to show them that they do matter, and I think that is the key.

> *We continually create reality by the language we use.*

Theme: LISTENING AND ANALYSIS

16. *I keep hearing a theme/message that...*
17. *A little while ago I thought I heard you say...then a little while later I thought I Heard you say...and now I'm hearing... How do we put all of this together? What do you think is going on?*

Leighanne Law, Library and English

In my English class, the students are writing "flash fiction" stories in various genres and are finalizing their fourth story. One of my students was puzzling out where to take his story—it was a fantasy—and, as we were conferencing, **I mentioned that I was hearing a theme in his writing**: people struggling with their perception of reality.

He told me that he had, at one very critical point in his life, dealt with that very issue and I asked him what it would be like for him to remix his own genre: fantasy mixed with personal narrative. He said he thought he would do that and began writing intently. Since that moment, his story has become even more powerful, chilling, and authentic.

Marjie Bowker, English

During a conference, a student and I were talking about his family's struggle with gaining legal status. He had been born in the U.S., but the rest of his family had been deported back to Mexico. He has been very successful at Scriber since he moved in with other family members; after not attending school for many years, he had entered the end of his sophomore year with no credits. Despite his success, his mind is usually on his family, whom he only gets to see once or twice a year when he goes to Mexico. He takes two weeks off of school to do this and slips a bit when he returns because he is so distracted.

I decided to focus on his situation rather than his slipping grades, so I said, **"It sounds like a lot of your life has been about uncertainty."**

He readily agreed, and we continued our conversation for about ten minutes about his family and what they meant to him. Eventually, we moved on to the topic of grades and effort.

"On a scale of one to ten, how important is earning your diploma?" I asked.

"A TEN!" he replied without hesitation. "It's why my parents sent me here, to succeed. It's my main reason for being apart from them."

We then moved on to discuss what he could do to catch up on missed work and improve his grades, but the importance of understanding his feelings about his family was a crucial part of understanding his whole situation.

Andrea Hillman, Associate Principal

I love how "Cal Crowing" a student is part of our lexicon at Scriber and that most staff use the 17 Questions regularly with students. One of the most courageous things I have noted is staff being brave enough to really get at the true student beneath the superficial student they present to the world. One of my operating principles in working with kids is "They don't care what you know until they know that you care." It is a risky thing for teachers to put themselves in a position to get to know a student at that level, and the beauty of having the 17 Questions is that there is a road map for teachers to be able to do that. These questions have scaffolded a way to have those meaningful conversations with kids. Even if you don't have a natural aptitude for communicating that way, you can always re-ground yourself by having the list of questions readily available.

Chapter Six

CHANGING CONVERSATIONS, PART THREE

Reflection

In *transactions*, people participate in activities and exchange information, but no one is changed very much, and neither are the systems they work in. "Hello, how's it going, great" is a transaction. In *transformations*, we have "aha" experiences that result in growth and change. We are not the same after transformative conversations, and neither are the systems we work within.

To take transformation to the next level, we want our students to be able to *describe the transformations they have experienced, and the implications of these for their lives*. In other words, we cultivate meta-cognition. We invite students to reflect on the process of shifting their focus to their dreams for the future. Through additional reflection, students develop even more resiliency—the capacity to solve problems, overcome obstacles, and rebound.

In most of the following interactions described, our staff was intentional about asking students how they felt about receiving a "Most Transformed Award" at our recognition assembly. It was a new award we piloted as a result of our *Your Future Now* work and we thought that these awards would give us the perfect opportunity to practice fostering meta-cognition. Our goal is to have our students reflect on all kinds of transformations in the days to come.

Pete Folta, Social Studies

The week leading up to the recognition assembly, I told N he needed to be at school on Wednesday. This really piqued his interest, and for the rest of the week, he kept coming by my room to "check in." Sometimes he would say "hi," and sometimes he would just give me a hard time.

When his name was called for the "Most Transformed" award, he walked up to the front of the auditorium, smiling all the way.

In my haste I had forgotten to sign the certificates, which weren't really much to look at. Over the years I had seen certificates very similar to these on the floor, under chairs, in wastebaskets and folded in half in backpacks.

However, N came in early the next morning and said (with certificate in perfect condition), "Hey, you need to sign this!"

"**How did it feel to win this award**?" I asked.

"I was surprised, because of what the award meant. I was proud of myself and glad that teachers noticed. I've never been noticed before."

"**Do you know why you got it?**"

"Because of my attitude change. I paid attention to my work and actually tried. It made me want to do even better."

Dave Zwaschka, English

D began the semester with inconsistent attendance, but as the weeks went on not only did his attendance improve, but so did his attitude and quality of work.

I saw him in the hall the day after the recognition assembly and asked him what it meant to have others recognize him for his hard work. He smiled sheepishly and said, "Pretty good," and continued to walk. Then he stopped, walked back towards me and said, "Really good. I put my certificate on my refrigerator."

> *All of our present interpretations of the universe are subject to revision or replacement.*
> – George Kelly

Mike Carey, Math

A few students tracked me down after the recognition assembly because they were shocked they didn't win the "Most Transformed" award. They recounted their feelings of disappointment and disbelief as they sat in the assembly and watched me present the award to another student. They said they felt robbed because they pictured me presenting the award to them.

One student explained that she had been one of the worst students in my class last year. This year, however, she planned to graduate and had worked very hard, harder than she ever had worked before. I agreed that she was equally deserving of the award, but explained that I had given it to a junior to inspire him to continue his good work.

Feeling badly, I asked if I could give her something else, and she said that money might help heal her hurt feelings. As I pulled a dollar bill out of my pocket, a huge smile broke out across her face. She was psyched and took the peace offering. Later, **I asked her how she felt** about "winning" in this unconventional manner. She told me that she had gone to McDonald's later that day with someone very important to her and had been able to buy fries with the dollar. She also got to explain the situation and it had made her very happy.

I also asked the student who won the award **to tell me how the recognition had made her feel**. She said it felt amazing to be recognized for her efforts. The award was evidence that she had impressed me, she explained, and the certificate validated her achievements. Best of all, she felt that the certificate would pave the way for her future success because she could highlight it when applying for jobs and college scholarships. I was surprised that a simple certificate would mean so much to such a talented and intelligent student. Everyone needs validation.

Michael Waldren, Science paraeducator

P is a quiet kid who rarely invests energy into anyone else. He occupies all extra class time with a laptop borrowed from the library.

However, when he received the "Most Transformed" award for science, his social capacity opened up. He spoke with other students about his achievement, and while he was directing jokes at the award, it was quite clear that it had a noticeable impact on him. Even though he was spouting statements along the lines of "I can't believe I got this award," the fact that he was discussing it with students clearly justified the choice to give it to him.

After he articulated his astonishment once more, I **asked him how he felt about receiving it**. After a moment of thought, he said it was a good feeling, despite the surprise element.

"Why did you feel surprised?"

He promptly brought up his typical anti-social demeanor, stating that he seldom interacts with others.

Once he shared that with me, I quickly countered, stating that his interaction with me was proof enough that his capacity to speak with others was highly intact.

It was apparent that P's self-esteem was positively impacted, and that the courage to speak to others was clearly in his veins.

Kanoe Vierra, Dean of Students, English and Entry

I spoke with one of my award recipients after the assembly. This student, who is very shy and quiet, was very appreciative and told me that it had "made her day."

When I asked her **how it felt to have been given the award**, she said she was grateful; more importantly, she had been given an opportunity to "come out of her shell," participate in small group discussions and to thrive in the classroom. I believe the response was a result of the activities we did in Steps to Success with the Entry Students and this particular student discovering her strengths, skills and talents over the course of the quarter.

Marjie Bowker, English

When J came to class after being recognized for "Most Transformed" in math at the recognition assembly, I said, "Congratulations!"

He responded with a really big smile.

"How does that feel?"

He said, "I'm going to hang this on my refrigerator."

"Do you know why you won this?"

"I'm finally taking school seriously!"

After T won an award for "Most Transformed" in English, I asked him, **"Do you know why you won that award?"**

"Kinda, yeah. I mean, I'm doing my work and I'm not slacking off anymore," he answered.

"How did it feel to win?"

Another huge smile. "It felt pretty good! I mean I was kind of shy about it. But I felt really good walking up to get it."

During V's student/teacher conference, I asked him how it felt to know that he would be graduating on time.

"It feels like I did the impossible," he said.

"Say more about that," I encouraged.

"Well, if anyone had told me when I came to this school that I would do this, I wouldn't have believed them."

"But you did it."

"Yeah! I have worked really hard."

"Wow, V, **how does that make you feel?"**

Big smile. "You have no idea!"

Zachary Taylor, College and Career Specialist

I informed a student that he was being honored as student of the month.

"YES!" he shouted.

"How does this make you feel?" I asked.

"I've been waiting for this moment my whole life!" he said.

Chapter Seven
MOTIVATIONAL INTERVIEWS

A frequent approach to addressing undesirable student behavior is to point to rules or policies and to remind students of what they will lose if they don't change. Research indicates that telling students to change their behavior is rarely effective. However, if adults can communicate in ways that help students recognize and own the need for change, they will get more positive results.

Motivational Interviewing is a counseling approach originally developed for professionals in the field of substance abuse. However, the principles can be applied in many other settings. For many students, certain sets of behaviors have almost taken on the characteristics of addictions, and have become habitual—such as skipping school. Intellectually, they know what they are doing is not good for them. They may tell themselves and others that it is only temporary, that it will be better or different "tomorrow," but they can't visualize their lives being much different than they are today.

As defined by its developers, "Motivational Interviewing is a directive, client-centered counseling style for eliciting behavior change by helping clients (students) to explore and resolve ambivalence."

Students behave as they do because they are receiving some kind of payoff for their behavior. From their perspective, this behavior is providing what they think they want or need. Motivational Interviewing focuses on talking with students in ways that help them to 1) reflect on their behavior choices, and 2) develop a readiness to change them. It is non-judgmental and non-confrontational. It recognizes that people are at different levels when it comes to making changes in their lives. It views the professional's role as one of listening, probing, reflecting and clarifying.

Our staff chose multiple students who seemed ambivalent about their futures for these interviews (which also utilize the 17 Questions—in bold). Cal and Marjie initiated the practice of conducting these interviews, and over time, more staff members participated and selected their own interviewees.

The following four interviews were led by Cal and assisted (and transcribed) by Marjie.

C—Cal

M—Marjie

S—Student

Student #1—October, 2014

Background: This student had shown remarkable growth over the past year. The previous spring he had been removed from regular classes and was placed in STEP (Student Transition Education Program); he couldn't stay in class or stay on task. But so far, he has been engaged in—and passing—his classes all semester. Our staff decided he would be a great candidate for motivational interviewing.

S walks in.

M—Hey, S, I was just filling Cal in on you a little bit, trying to describe you to him.

C—Hi, S. Nice to meet you. How would you describe yourself?

S—Well, I'm more of an outdoor kind of person. I prefer the woods to being in school.

C—**Please say more about that.**

S—I've grown up fishing and hunting my whole life—it's something my whole family does.

C—Where do you hunt?

S—Vantage, Poulsbo. I got my first deer in Poulsbo.

C—First deer?

S—Only deer.

C—Where do you fish?

S—Neah Bay. I just learned how to fly fish at Lost Lake. We also go to Quincy.

C—I'm from that area.

S—So you are familiar with the lakes there?

C—Very familiar! How often do you get to do that?

S—Twice a year.

(This conversation continues.)

C—**What do you plan to do in your future?**

S—My family is in the HVAC business, so I can join that. Or I can go to college for Fish and Game, but that would take me six years, so I'm not sure. But a bunch of my family members have broken their backs in the HVAC business, so I don't really want to do it.

M—Having a job outdoors would be perfect for you, I'm guessing.

S—Yeah, definitely. But I don't want to go to school for six years.

C—What are your favorite subjects?

S—Biology. Math—I wish it was easier, though. My teacher has been out and we've had a sub, so I don't understand anything.

C—What happens when you don't understand?

S—I get pissed off and stop working. I go by respect. If a teacher respects me, I respect them. If they do something to make me mad, I get them back.

C—**It sounds like "getting back" is a theme with you.**

S—Yes.

C—If I'm a teacher, how do you want me to treat you?

S—I want you to say please.

C—How has the "If you respect me, I'll respect you" approach worked for you?

S—Well, it makes some teachers more mad.

C—**Sounds like** there's a power struggle going on. Someone has to win or lose.

S—Yeah.

C—Is that something we can work on?

S—Yeah. Probably.

C—In the workplace, people get fired because of personality issues and power struggles.

S—Yeah, I know.

C—If you're a forest worker, people will view you as someone they are paying with their taxes. How would you handle their disrespect?

S—I would be professional.

C—**What would you say if I told you that you could get into Fish and Game in less than 6 years?**

S—I would like that. Yes, my family wants me to do that. They want me to look into it.

C—Did you know there is a lot of information about that career available to you?

S—Yeah.

C—It's possible you could get a scholarship. I have a friend who is setting up a scholarship for that right now.

S—Yes, but my grandma has done well financially, so she set up a scholarship fund for me. I can use it to study any field in wildlife and conservation.

C—That's great. How is school going for you right now?

S—I like school. Other people distract me, though. I like it here better than other schools.

C—How's it different?

S—Smaller classes, more attention. We know the teachers.

C—A lot of teachers have noticed a real change in you this year.

S—Yes, I guess I have changed. I'm doing better.

M—Specifically, Peter has mentioned that you're doing really well.

S—Yeah, Peter and I didn't get along before, but now we do. It's really good now.

C—**How does it feel to hear that teachers are saying this about you?**

S—That's really cool.

(He needs to text someone to get a ride and go home.)

S—I think I have to go now, my ride is leaving.

C—I would like to set up another meeting with you, if you've found this worthwhile.

S—Definitely. I would like that.

C—Is there anything you want to ask me/us?

S—Yeah, you should talk to your friend about that scholarship and see when it will be available.

C—**It seems like you are really interested** in pursuing this.

S—Yes, I really love the outdoors. My family, we will pick up garbage left by other people. We really care about the environment. My cousin and I used to fish together, but he died because of drinking. He went around a corner too fast... That's why I'm not drinking anymore. At least not very much.

C—He died instantly, just like that, on impact?

S—Yes.

C—I'm sorry.

S—Well, I have to go, but yeah, let me know when we can talk again.

(shakes Marjie's hand, shakes Cal's hand)

NEXT DAY: Marjie sees him in the hall and—after looking up "Game Warden" the day before—calls him in before school to take a look at the WOIS information because the requirements are less than six years. He looks at the skills needed, the job description, etc. He says, "This all fits me. Can you write me a note to come back during Silent Reading so I can read more?"

SSR: He comes back and spends twenty minutes looking at colleges, the job outlook, the pay, etc. and tells Marjie (with excitement) about what is required—it seems doable for him. Marjie mentions that now that he knows where the programs are, maybe he could apply for some scholarships.

S—That sounds good, but my grandma has money for me.

M—What happens to that money if you get scholarships?

S—I get it when I'm 21.

M –That sounds like a good deal. By the way, college is more expensive than you think!

S—Yes, I've heard that. OK, thanks for showing me all of that, Marjie. That is cool.

Second Meeting, following week:

C—How have things been going since we last talked?

S—Good. I've been really busy taking care of my sister's baby.

C—We didn't talk about that last time. **Tell me more about that.**

(S explains that he is in charge of child care after school)

C—Last time we talked about your changes and transformations. What other changes have you noticed?

S—I'm definitely doing better in all of my classes. Except math. My teacher has been out and all of the subs teach differently. It's hard.

*(He tells us that he read his first book on his own (other than in class)—one that Peter gave him—*Enrique's Journey. *He describes what he liked about it, says it repeated a lot but that it was a good story.)*

M—**How did it feel to finish a book on your own time?**

S—It felt good.

C—What's your next book?

S—Probably something my dad gives me. I like fiction better.

M—I was telling Cal that you got on the WOIS system last week and learned more about what it takes to be a game warden.

C—Yes, how was that?

S—It was really good. It's good that it only takes two years. I talked to my friend's mom—she's a Seattle cop—and she says that game wardens get the same training they do because a lot of people in the woods are meth addicts.

C—Yes, that's true. People on the lam go to the woods. You also need some college training. Did you find information on that?

S—Yes, pretty much any college has these programs.

C—**How would you feel about** finding out some more specific information? Would you like that?

S—Yea, that would be good. I talked to my mom about it and she is happy. She's telling me to do it.

M—You talked to her this past week?

S—Yeah.

M—And she wants you to do what you're passionate about?

S—Yeah, and she says I can live at home and go to college.

C—That's really nice to know! It seems to me that you've changed more than just in Peter's class. You just read your first book. How are your other subjects?

(We begin talking about English last year. He didn't really like The Fault in Our Stars *because it was too much of a "girl book." But he liked* Fahrenheit 451. *We talked about that book for a minute...)*

S—I like to read, but I can't write. I can't write at all. I could never write an essay.

M—S, you did write some things last year. I remember the poem you wrote.

S—Yeah, I did write that. But, well, that's...

M—You just said you can't do it, but you did. **How did you feel about it after you did it?**

S—Really good.

M—You wrote it about your cousin (who died last spring in an accident involving alcohol). It was a really good poem.

S—Did you show it to Kathy?

M—No, I didn't. But I'm sure she would love to see it.

S—I have it here in my wallet.

M—Really? You keep it in your wallet?

(He fishes around and takes out a few things before he finds it.)

M—I had no idea! Can Cal read it?

(While Cal reads the poem, we keep talking)

M—**When did you decide** you couldn't write?

S—I've never been able to, since forever.

M—At what point do you get frustrated?

S—Right away. I know what I want to say, but can't get it down.

M—Have you ever been tested for that?

S—Never.

C—*(After reading the poem)* Very effective. I could visualize all of this happening.

(S smiles.)

C—One thing to keep in mind about ranger work is that it requires a lot of writing. It has to hold up in court, so it must be well written. Fred has talked about that, all the writing that is involved in his job.

M—S, I will probably have you for English again next semester. **What would you say if I told you that I believe you will be able to write essays?**

S—*(smiles)* That sounds great. Yeah. I want to be able to.

M—That is what we will work on—building your confidence. Because you did write, and you wrote well. We will work on improving your skills. We don't want this to get in the way of the career you want.

S—Right.

C—I know you have to go now, but would you have time to go to the career center and learn more about the job you want?

S—Yes, definitely. Thank you. I'll see you next time.

(He shakes both of our hands again.)

Note: This student did spend some more time checking into this career with Zach in the Career Center. Most importantly, it became part of our ongoing discussion throughout the year.

Student #2, January, 2015

Background: Cal and Marjie had only 20 minutes with this student because he had to catch a bus to Everett to discuss a possible housing situation. He had come to Scriber knowing he wanted to be a firefighter, but a lot of life hardships had gotten in the way—including homelessness—and he was losing vision for his future. We knew it was crucial to meet with him because he had become despondent.

(After S and Cal are introduced, they begin talking about his appointment for temporary housing...)

C—Have you given any thought to when you get out of school? What sounds interesting to do for a job?

S—I guess with everything that's been going on, I just want to take it day by day.

C—Let's take a minute and talk about the future, is that OK?

S—Sure.

C—Let's say you are settled into your new place—you have all of that taken care of. What can you see yourself doing at that point?

S—I don't know. Everything depends on this new place. I don't want to be there very long because it's going to be strict and it will change everything.

C—How would it change your life?

S—I can only be out eight nights per month.

C—So what kind of place is it?

S—The Friends of Youth.

C—I'm familiar with that. Well, as you think about all the things people are doing out there—have you considered something that you might like to do?

S—The only thing I've thought of is going to Community College to study firefighting but I'm not sure anymore.

C—**What happened to change that**?

S—I've heard it's really hard. I've heard you have to be one of the best, that it's really competitive. So if I need something immediately…

C—**What was the attraction in the beginning**?

S—The thrill of it, the thought of saving someone.

M—The first thing I knew about him was his desire to become a firefighter.

C—So you say the thrill? Helping people, saving people? **What other areas** would give the same pay off?

S—Maybe a cop, hands on work.

C—Like what?

S—I don't want to be behind a desk. Would lose my mind.

C—Could you do something like Marjie does—become a teacher?

S—Yeah, maybe. But I don't like talking in front of everyone. Never thought about it.

C—You would certainly be helping people…**what would you think about** doing some exploration on some of the possibilities available to you when you're out of school?

S—It's probably a good idea. I haven't looked into it much.

C—A lot of interesting careers out there. Do you know how many there are?

S—Not really.

C—Just about a thousand. Most people know only a few of them—20 or 30. That's what we are trying to do at SLHS, explore some possibilities. The reason this is important is that if you have this idea about "future" then the things you are doing now could have more meaning.

(*pause*)

C—Can you respond to that?

S—I don't know. I mean I have also looked into the military, but I don't like the idea of leaving everything behind. But I thought that when I graduate, I might see how many reasons I have to stay.

C—How many reasons do you have now to stay?

S—Couple friends and my girlfriend.

C—OK. I thought your statement that you would have to consider how many people you would have to leave behind was a good statement. I'm guessing you have thought about that before?

(*long silence, tears*)

C—**Can I ask what's going on right now**?

S—I don't know, it's just… I can't really say.

C—**What would you think about doing some serious planning for your future?** The military? How much exploring have you done?

S—Well, that's more just like someplace to stay. With benefits.

C—Did you know they have firefighters in the military? Almost everything that exists in the civilian world exists there. What did you want to do there?

S—I'm not sure. I thought I would just take a test.

C—Well it depends on many things. Sometimes they will guarantee you a school. They will sign a deal and you can get the training you want. **What do you think about that?**

S—Well, yeah, but military is a last resort for me because I would have to leave everyone behind.

C—What if you didn't have to do that?

S—Well, I don't want to come back and have everything be different from when I left.

M—S, didn't we look up firefighting on WOIS and look into similar careers? What happens when you start looking through that?

S—I feel like I'm just looking through options.

C—**Could you say more about that?**

S—Well, when I'm looking, I'm not thinking about myself. I'm just looking at random careers.

C—So it's not connecting at all?

S—No.

C—**What would it take to change that,** so that you could be looking at those and connect it to yourself?

S—I guess I just need to take it more seriously.

C—What if it wasn't just that? What if there were people who could assist you in that search? Because I agree with you that if you're just reading through it, it's not helping. You're getting information, but nothing more.

S—I mean, yeah, it's probably a good idea.

C—**What would you think about doing that?**

S—Yeah, I should probably just make myself do it.

M—Have you met Zach? The career guy?

S—Oh, he watches us play basketball.

C—You like basketball?

S—Yeah, just shoot at lunch.

C—I'm not sure if you know why I'm here. I'm with a project called *Your Future Now* and we're trying to make sure that each student here is looking at a possible future instead of just looking for credits and diploma. We said "there's got to be more than just that." We want everyone to know what the next step might be after graduation.

M—I would be so happy to see you leaving here with a goal. When you first came you had this clear direction. I want to help you get to that place before you leave. The excitement that you had for that goal.

C—**Could you say more about the excitement?**

S—At the time it looked like something fun to do as a career. But then I realized it wouldn't be as easy as I was expecting it to be.

C—Can I give you some feedback? The things that you have described to me—**it sounds like** you've been through a lot that hasn't been easy.

S—Yeah, well, not so much that as that. It's so hard to get the job. In my case, I need something immediate. After high school I only have myself.

(long pause, trying to control tears)

C—You seem to me like a pretty "with it" guy who has it together. You're pretty strong. So when you say "I only have myself," I would put that in a positive way. You can say "I have myself. Let's look at the possibilities."

(still unable to respond)

M—You have a lot of people who care about you here.

S—I know I'm going to have to support myself.

C—I'm wondering if there's a part of you that wonders if you are up to that job.

S—Yeah, I guess. It's going to be weird and hard, but I need to do it.

C—But you have a lot of support. Probably a lot more than others in your situation. I realize you need to catch a bus, but what might the next step be? Would you be up for talking to Zach?

S—I don't want to take a bunch more tests.

M—I will make sure it's not about tests.

C—Can we ask him to contact you?

S—Yeah.

C—He will do the same as we've done here. But he can direct you. Maybe there are scholarships.

M—I will write him an email today. You can meet with him during Silent Reading.

C—Would you like to continue this discussion?

S—Yeah, it's been beneficial to me.

Zachary Taylor, Career Center—follow up, next day

For many months I would see this student, headphones on, smile unseen. I had heard the backstory about his family—he was all alone, living independently. Most people would just shut down, but he kept coming to school. Cal and Marjie interviewed him and sent him my way. I was excited to work with him.

I asked about his plan and he said wanted to go into fire service. He heard it was really hard and he wondered how he would pay for it. I explained the financial aid process, and then we went on to filing his FAFSA. Because he was considered independent, we needed no additional information. Within twenty minutes we had finished his FAFSA.

"You qualify for $5,700 in grants, money you won't have to pay back. That will cover your tuition at a Community College," I explained.

A few seconds passed until he processed the news. "Awesome!" he said with a half-smile, but that was the most amount of joy I had ever seen him express. We talked about Fire Service at Everett CC and about him becoming an EMT and gaining experience while also getting paid. The discussion changed from something he might do to something he is going to do—once he understood the process.

Since this discussion I have seen him with his headphones off during lunch, smiling (half smile), interacting with other people.

Student #3, November, 2014

Background: This student has a really great sense of humor; our staff often laughs about how sometimes we don't get his dry jokes until minutes after he comments on something. But every time he's asked about his future, he either responds with "I don't know" or makes a joke out of the "Steps to Success" (Chapter Ten) activity in Family. We decided he would be a great candidate to interview.

(Cal walks in while I'm talking to S.)

M—I was just telling S a little bit about you and what we'll be talking about today.

C—What did you think about what you heard?

S—Sounds good to me. Interesting.

M—So, S has been here for a while. He may win a prize for being here the longest.

S—I've been here for three or four years.

C—How much more time do you have here?

S—I should be graduating this year. I have a couple of credits to go.

C—**How do you feel about that?**

S—A little scared. School is about the only thing I have going.

C—**Say more about that.**

S—I don't have a job and it's going to be hard for me to find a job because of the body modifications I've done.

C—Can you say more about that? Because **it sounds like it's important.**

S—Well, I've worked in quite a few places. Nowadays, lots of people judge you because of the way you look. People might think I am up to no good. Plus, I get very nervous when it comes to interviews.

C—Are you nervous now?

S—A little bit.

C—You mentioned the jobs you've had. Have you thought at all about the next 30 years of your life? Five years? What do you want to be doing?

S—Working, living on my own. I haven't put much thought into my future. There are some things I'm interested in, though.

C—Like what?

S—Comedy, I like to make people laugh. Maybe even acting. I feel I can BS my emotions really well. Also, I've come to find that I really like to cook as well.

C—So how could you move into one of those areas, at least explore one of them?

S—I know there's culinary school.

C—What do you like about cooking?

S—Making delicious things. I love to eat. I'm a picky eater. There's nothing better than to cook something for myself or someone else who appreciates it. It boosts my confidence up.

M—What have you made that someone really liked?

S—I made beef pot pie and that turned out to be really fricking good. I made it by myself. Cheesecake bites, chili. It was delicious.

C—Do you follow recipes?

S—Yes, but I also have experiences from my dad. We're Hispanic and I ask about how to do some things.

C—How would you feel about looking into one of these programs?

S—I would be up for that. But, like I said, I'm not too sure about it. I'm a really picky eater. If I cook something I don't like and they say I have to try it, I wouldn't want to.

C—So let's assume you move into this area and you become a cook. You would have to cook a lot of different things.

S—As long as I don't have to try it.

C—Are you aware of schools in the area?

S—No, I have no knowledge of it.

C—Would you be interested in doing that?

S—Well, I'm still not sure. I'm still bouncing around a lot. During my ninth grade year, I got into a lot of trouble and I didn't care about anything. I had a really bad attitude. It wasn't until I came here that I started to change. The teachers here kind of brought out the best in me.

C—**What would you think about** exploring the culinary schools in this area?

S—I would be OK with that.

C—Some of the best ones are at the community colleges. Did you know that?

S—No, I didn't. I'm worried about the money part. My parents aren't making very much money right now.

C—Have you talked to your parents about this?

S—No, I have always been really stubborn and I told my parents that I just wanted to go into the workforce and hopefully get lucky.

C—I heard you say earlier that you were afraid that people would dismiss you because of your appearance.

S—Yes, it's because all of this stuff (piercings) doesn't look professional.

C—How do you see yourself getting job in light of this fear that you mentioned?

S—Well, I have a lot of friends who look just like me who have gone out and gotten jobs that they enjoy. I just have to find the right place and be motivated. I'm not too thrilled about the idea of having to go out and get a job and pay bills.

C—That's one of the reasons I'm here is to help students make that transition. What do you have in the way of strengths, skills and talents that you could market?

S—I'm good at physical labor.

C—**I heard you say** you didn't want to do that.

S—Yes, but that's what I've done. Mostly labor and cleaning for family. I didn't like having family telling me what to do. They aren't my bosses, they're my family. I don't want to do something that I hate.

C—What do you do when you don't have anything to do?

S—I'm trying to learn the guitar.

C—You have one?

S—Yes, my dad has an acoustic and an electric. My little sister has a ukulele. I like to draw.

C—Like what?

S—Just things I see. From websites. It's something I'm working on.

C—Do you ever draw things that just come out of your head?

S—Not really. I'm not too skilled. My sister is really talented and seeing her do that made me want to pursue that. She's not going to school because she doesn't have her papers. I do, though. I was born here. She was born in Tijuana.

C—We want to make sure you're ready for the next step from here. How could we best do that?

S—Well, I have a pretty good idea of how the world works. I've been living with a family that's been struggling for a long time. I'm aware of what it will be like if I don't get my life together. I've seen people keep a child mindset.

C—What are some examples of that?

S—Well, my brother. He dropped out of high school. My parents kicked him out at a very young age. He's been in and out of jail, in a gang, doing hard drugs. He's homeless at the moment. It's really horrible to see him like that.

C—I was just going to ask...what is it like to see your brother like that? What does that do to you?

S—Well, uh, it hurts. *(has trouble speaking, tears up, long pause.)* Yeah. *(Another long pause.)*

C—**What I'm hearing from you** is "I've seen that and I don't want that."

S—Yes.

C—So what could we do to help?

S—Point me in the right direction because I don't know.

C—And that's why we're here. What's it like to say "I need help" and "I don't know"?

S—It sucks. I've been through things like that before. I was expelled in ninth grade because I got involved in a lot of shit. I had to go through a lot of court. It opened my eyes to what life could be like.

C—**Let me share what I'm hearing.** You know you don't want that, or what happened to your brother, but you're not sure what to do.

S—Yeah. I have changed significantly this past year, though.

C—What is the greatest change you have noticed?

S—My attitude. I went from being super negative and angry to being outgoing and trying to see how to make things better for myself.

C—What are the best parts of you?

S—The way I communicate with people.

C—What else?

S—*(Long pause.)* If I have a passion for something, I'm going to stick to it no matter how many times I fail.

C—What is your passion? What do you want to be doing?

S—Like I said, acting would be at the top of my list.

C—What is there about that?

S—The way someone can pretend to be someone else and be good at it. I see the way actors do things and it's really believable the way they do it.

M—Do you look at that and say "I can do that?"

S—Yes. People don't ever know if I'm being serious or joking around.

C—What would it take to get you into something like that?

S—I don't know.

C—Would you be interested?

S—Yes, definitely. But I really don't have high hopes for the future.

C—You don't' have high hopes? Where is that coming from?

S—From me. That's just how I think it's going to be. *(Tears up.)* No one ever tells me not to do things. My parents are very supportive and let me do whatever. I don't really like to think about the future.

M—**What made you decide** that you don't have high hopes?

S—The more I'm stuck in the future, the more I think I'll miss out on today. Today is what I'm worried about.

C—**What would it take** so that you had high hopes?

S—Find something in myself that I see worthwhile. Because all of my current dreams that I have aren't really too certain. And they wouldn't pay too well unless I was really good at them.

C—This is the first time I've heard you mention your dreams. **Could you say more about that?**

S—What do you mean?

C—Well, I heard you talk about your dreams. A dream means you have some kind of picture of what you want.

S—I just want to be happy.

C—When are you happiest?

S—When I'm not home. When I'm with my friends. They're truly the only people who understand me for me. At home I have to hold back a little of who I am. At school I can be myself. *(Tears up again, long pause.)*

C—What are you thinking right now?

S—My mind is blank now.

C—Nothing there?

S—Like I said, I really haven't put much thought into things until this year. I realized I'm going to be out of this place and now I need to figure it out.

C—You realize you have to do something.

S—Yes, my parents are going to expect me to work. So I spent all last summer working.

C—At a job you didn't like?

S—Yes, I had to stay in Everett. The only time I could go out was on the weekends. It was really crappy.

C—**What I hear you saying** is that your life wasn't your own. It belonged to somebody else.

S—Mostly because my parents and my uncle don't trust me. They look at me as someone who goes out and gets into trouble.

C—How would you like them to think about you? What would you want them to be saying if they were over in the corner talking about you?

S—That they're proud of me. That they like me for me.

C—What would make that happen?

S—The only goal I have right now is to graduate high school.

C—How would you feel if we started here by giving you some information, some ideas. Not taking over at all. **What I hear you saying** right now is that you're scared and aren't quite sure how to get control of that. For example, if you were to get information about acting or culinary arts, comedy?

M—You're also a very funny writer.

S—Am I?

C—**What's it like** to have your teacher tell you you're a funny writer?

S—*(smiles)* It's good.

M—S has a way of twisting things in a really fresh, funny way.

S—It's scary to me, though, the idea of failing.

C—What's scary about it?

S—The feeling of it.

C—Have you decided that you're a failure in some things?

S—Yes, in some ways. I mean there are some things I'm not good at and I fail at those things.

C—But if you could focus on the things you're best at?

S—But that's hard because I don't do very many things. I'm just home most of the time. I'm stuck there taking care of my sisters. I don't have much free time. The free time I have I take full advantage of. I don't have money to do things.

C—If you had money how would you spend it?

S—I would move out as quickly as possible.

C—What else?

S—Buy myself things.

C—Like what?

S—More jewelry. Good jewelry, gold with actual diamonds.

C—What's the attraction about the jewelry?

S—It makes me feel good about myself. I can express myself. I don't look good with them off. It's confidence. It makes me feel good about myself. I get a lot of compliments from people.

C—What about your family?

S—They don't like it. They are traditional Hispanics. My sister is a lesbian, and my uncles don't like that. They said some pretty bad things. They've said bad things about the way I look, too. I went to the food bank with my mom the other day and there was a lady in line who started talking about my piercings. She was talking to my mom and my mom defended me. I wanted to tell that lady to shut up.

C—**What would you think about** working with Marjie and other people here so that when you leave here, you will have some kind of a plan?

S—Sure. I mean I want some kind of job. If it means getting experience, I'll do a crappy job for a while so I can get a bigger idea of what I might like to do with my life. I haven't done much with my life yet because I haven't had the opportunity to do many things since my family has struggled for so long.

C—What would you think about working while you are taking a class? You could be taking math, psychology, while you're working. How would you like something like that?

S—I wouldn't like it. I don't want to take psychology. I'm not interested in that. I wish there was a way to just study one thing without taking all of those other things I don't care about.

M—**Sounds like** you want something really specific and focused?

S—Yes.

M—That's something really good to know, so you don't waste time. There are many programs that focus on one thing, like culinary arts programs. You want something creative, specific.

S—Yes.

C—Do you want to pursue some information on culinary arts?

S—Yes, that would be good.

C—Thanks a lot. We'll let you get on your way. Would you like to meet again?

S—Sure, at another time.

M—We'll get Mike involved in the discussion during S2S. We'll make it an ongoing discussion this year.

S—OK, thanks. *(Shakes Cal's hand and then mine.)*

We met with student #3 again a few months later. He reacted with enthusiasm about meeting again; however, he had made little progress regarding his future goals, despite lots of staff intervention and invitations. This next part comes at the end of the second interview:

C—**Here's what I'm hearing you say**: "I really don't trust myself. Here are the rules and regulations, but I don't trust myself." Is that accurate?

S—Yes, that's very accurate.

C—**How would you feel if we could change that?** Would you be willing to explore how to do that?

S—Well, it's kind of in my nature now.

C—Part of it's in your nature, but another thing I heard you say is "I don't like people telling me what to do." **So on the one hand, "I don't like people telling me what to do" and on the other hand "as long as I do what other people tell me to do, I'm safe. I don't get into trouble."**

S—If I had a job and someone told me exactly what to do, I'd be perfectly fine with that. So perfectly fine if they said, "Do this, then do that."

C—Suppose it was a job you didn't like.

S—I'm fine with that, as long as there was no way of screwing things up. I don't like screwing things up.

C—I think that's probably a good place to stop—I know you need to get back to class. **What did you think of our conversation today?**

S—It was good.

C—**What was the best thing about it?**

S—You telling me in words how I am because I don't really have people telling me.

C—Really?

S—Yeah, like how I am or the way I feel—everything I said.

M—He held a mirror up to you.

S—Yeah.

C—Would you like to meet again?

S—Sure.

M—How much contact do you have with Zach (career specialist)?

S—Not that much.

M—What if we set up an appointment for you to explore some jobs and careers—some of your passions—to see what is available?

S—I'm focused more on jobs than an education.

M—He can help you with that, too.

C—The more options you have, the better off you will be down the line. We want to make sure you know what they are so you are choosing from a bunch of stuff.

S—Yeah, I get it. Sure, I'll do that.

C—OK, well it was nice talking to you.

(They shake.)

Student #4, September, 2014

Background: This student is capable of tearing a class apart in no time. He has been expelled, suspended, sent out, encouraged, mentored and talked to. However, we all love him; we don't know of another student we like more who has been more trouble. One day he posted this message on Facebook: *"I can't wait for school. I'm tired of the kids these days saying oh f#&* school.... No it's school and it's your future.*

Cal said, "Let's interview him." So we did.

C—Do you know why you're here?

S—The Facebook post?

C—What was behind that?

S—It bugged me that my friends said that.

C—When I heard that, I said, "Here's someone who gets it, that your future is important."

S—My father lives from paycheck to paycheck. I don't want to be like him.

C—What do you want to do?

S—I want to market stuff and talk to big corporate people.

C—**What do you like about it?**

S—It makes me feel big and important.

C—Your post makes me think you have leadership potential. **How does it feel** to hear me say that?

S—Good. I coach football at Richmond. My little brother's team.

C—There was a point you decided that was what you wanted to do. How did you decide that?

S—Have always loved football and would rather coach than play.

C—What are three things you like about coaching?

S—Having fun with kids, jumping in to play, they love me.

C—What is your response when they ask you to listen?

S—"Bring it!" I ask them all about what they're talking about.

C—You care?

S—Yes. I helped the quarterback lose five pounds by wrapping him in Saran Wrap and staying with him all night to make sure he didn't eat.

C—What about here at school"? What do you like?

S—Making people happy, jokes, putting people in a good mood.

C—The people who bother you, what about their complaints?

S—They think the whole system is messed up. Lots of students feel that way.

C—As a leader, how do you respond?

S—Ask questions, find out why. Bullying needs to be taken care of.

C—Are there things we could do?

S—Suspend people. We have to be harsh.

C—Will that solve the problem?

S—Maybe.

C—What could we do so that they care?

S—Bring Saturday School back.

C—Other things?

S—Find out what they care about.

C—How?

S—Dig into their lives.

C—Is that doable?

S—Yes, it would be hard, though.

C—Back to your post. The person who wrote this has leadership qualities. **How would you like** to be a part of the solution?

S—Yes, definitely. I used to get picked on. People tell me I'm annoying all the time.

C—**How does that make you feel**?

S—I brush it off.

C—If it's an issue, we need to look at it. How do we make people care about being here?

S—Ask questions, listen.

C—Talk to individuals? As a school? What if you did that?

S—Depends. Sometimes people get mad when you call them on things.

C—What would make students have a reason to come?

S—If you asked them what is in their future, then help them with their plan. They need to want to do it.

C—What is your favorite part of school?

S—Expressing myself in writing.

C—The students who don't like to be here—what is their reason?

S—They don't have trust. They need someone to trust here.

C—What triggered the change in your attitude toward school?

S—My dad and what he always says to me. I don't want to be like him.

C—**What do you think about** being told you are a leader—about us wanting you to find ways to help the school?

S—I would like to be a leader.

C—Do you feel the transformation of how you used to feel to now?

S—Yes, I feel it.

C—You seem like a role model. **How does that feel?**

S—It feels good. I'm making an impact on their lives (football team). I want them to have a good life.

C—So S is making a positive impact?

S—Yes.

C—You'd like to see more students make a contribution to school, is that right?

S—That's what I want to get across to people.

C—What is your main strength, skill, talent?

S—I'm outgoing and like to reach out.

(Bell rings.)

C—I hope to continue this conversation another time, S. Thanks for taking time to talk to us.

S—Thank you. Nice to meet you. *(They talk about the Husky game...)*

Second interview, two weeks later:

C—How are things going?

S—Good, I was accepted into Fire Service.

C—What did you have to do to get accepted?

S—Just apply.

C—**How did you decide** you wanted to do that?

S—T asked me and I thought it would be fun. I need to be active.

C—What do you do?

S—Today we worked on rolling up hoses. It was exhausting.

(talked about this for a while)

C—Last time we talked you expressed an interest in becoming a leader here and in your future. What has happened with that?

S—I don't know. I've been really overwhelmed.

C—What has the stress been doing to you?

S—No sleep. Aggravation.

C—**Say more about that.**

S—*(He mentions a frustrating family situation—that he doesn't feel "listened to.")*

C—How do you let this frustration out?

S—Get mad, punch walls.

C—How does it come out at school?

S—I'm loud. I swear.

C—What's going on in your mind when this is happening?

S—I try not to think about things too much. I just do it.

C—**Say more about that.**

S—*(He goes into more depth about not wanting to feel things.)*

C—Can you imagine a time when you could say "I can put this aside, I can go to school and create a better life down the line"?

S—I think so.

C—**What would it feel like** to be contributing as a leader, making school separate from what's happening at home so that you can make a life and future for yourself? We already know what you don't want...

S—I would like that. Yeah, that would feel good.

C—**What would it take** to make that happen?

S—To accept that I can't change what's going on at home.

C—That's part one, what's part two?

S—Come here, do my work, be serious about school.

C—**What if you said**, "I'm going to do my work and take a leadership role"?

S—I would feel good. I feel good when I help people.

C—**What would it take** for you to move into a leadership role?

S—Do my work?

C—What else? What motivates you?

S—Put my heart into it. Get all A's.

C—What would that do for you?

S—It would make me happy. I'd be successful. I could get scholarships.

C—If your heart was in it?

S—It would feel good to meet my goals.

C—**On a scale from 1-10, how important is it to leave all of this behind and move forward?**

S—A ten. Really important.

C—**What would help you to do that?**

S—Having someone to talk to, to get things out.

C—**I sense a hesitancy** with your response. Do you have questions about whether you'll be able to do this?

S—Yes.

C—**Say more about that.**

S—I always doubt myself. Sometimes I hate doing things because I don't want to screw up. If I'm not going to be perfect, why even try?

C—**How did you decide** that you had to be perfect?

S—Not sure.

C—Have you ever done anything positive where it's been good enough?

S—At home, no. Nothing is ever good enough. Some things at school. But then I still want to go for a better score.

C—**What would it take** for you to say "I'm good enough"?

S—Better self-esteem.

C—You are bright, and you have a lot to offer. You want to help people. What would it take to be able to say "I'm OK?"

S—It would be cool if I could do that.

M—S, you are more than OK. I appreciate it when you are just being you, like you are now, like when you wrote that poem last year. When you are you, people respect you and listen to you.

C—**How does it feel to hear her say that?**

S—It feels really good.

C—How many other people do you connect with?

S—None.

C—**How does it feel** to know that people enjoy connecting with you? That there are a lot of people who would like to connect with you?

S—Really good.

C—I have a feeling that not many people get to see this side of you.

S—No.

C—But it's there and very real.

S—Yes.

C –Thanks for talking to us, S. I hope that this conversation will help you as you make decisions in your life.

S—It has. Thank you. *(Shakes Cal's hand.)*

C—Thank you.

Note: Student #4 continued to be the student we both loved and dreaded, but our whole staff felt more connected after hearing his thoughtful responses in this interview. He will graduate this year and we hope that we've made a difference in his life.

Chapter Eight
QUESTION CLUB

During the first two years of the grant, we talked about "Cal's 17 Questions" (see Chapter Five) at many staff meetings and heard multiple stories of how these questions had been used by Cal and other educators/youth workers. Even though we loved the stories and really wanted to experience similar results, many of us just couldn't grasp how to go about changing our own conversations.

We decided to try placing the questions right in front of us while talking with students. This worked to some degree, but we often found ourselves overwhelmed regarding which direction to take.

This year we decided we needed to try a new approach. At first we asked students for permission to share their motivational interviews, recorded by various teachers, as scripts in staff meetings where we "acted" them out (see Chapter Seven). This was valuable, but still—we needed something more. What if we could come together and actually practice asking each other heart and soul questions in the Appreciative Inquiry/Motivational Interviewing styles? Then perhaps we could get a sense of the flow, receive feedback and build collegiality all at the same time. The "Cal Crow Question Club" was born.

Our first club meetings focused entirely on questioning each other. We separated into triads: one person played the role of "interviewer," one person the "interviewee," and one person observed the conversation and gave feedback at the end. The results worked. In fact, no one wanted to leave the first meeting because we were learning so much about each other. We also felt empowered as we gained confidence in our new roles as active listeners. We realized we didn't have to work very hard, especially if we first and foremost focused on asking each other to **please say more about that** when we were curious about something.

As Cal pointed out, the Common Core learning standards regularly focus on "drilling down." Students are required to operate at higher level thinking skills of analysis, synthesis and evaluation. Students are asked to explain their work. (How did you decide to do it this way rather than that way? What evidence do you have that this is a reasonable answer? How is this similar/connected to something you have learned before?) The Question Club allowed us to "drill down" on each other's lives.

We used the first three questions listed below for our first three Question Club meetings and then went on to use the club time to make contributions for this book. The rest of the questions are included because we hope they will be used to encourage more open dialogues among educators.[1]

1. What is your favorite thing to do when you don't have to do anything?
2. What is the most important thing for others to know about you?
3. Think of an educator you've had who made a difference in your life. What were the qualities of that person that affected you?
4. Besides the desire for fame and fortune, what happened to make you want to become an educator?
5. How has your experience thus far met or exceeded your expectations?
6. How does who you are in your deepest truth match with what you do in your job?
7. How long have you been in education? What is the greatest change you've noticed in your career?
8. What are your strengths as an educator?
9. What is a challenging situation you've had with a student—one that you wish you had handled more effectively?
10. What is an important lesson you've learned that you would want to pass on to those who are new to the profession?
11. What is an emotionally challenging event that has happened in your classroom experience?

---

1 These questions were developed in collaboration with Rick Stevenson of The School of Life Project. All rights reserved.

12. What is a meaningful event that has happened in the classroom—one that has stayed with you?
13. If you could change one thing to improve the educational system, what would it be?
14. What is your greatest worry, insecurity or fear about your job? Does anything in particular cause you to lay awake at night?
15. If you had three teacher wishes (and no you can't have more wishes), how would you spend them?

For question #1, (*What is your favorite thing to do when you don't have to do anything?*) we used even more specific questions to set us up to be excellent listeners:

That sounds interesting. Could you say a bit more about that?
How did that come about? What triggered that interest?
What makes this enjoyable/satisfying?
What did you have to do to learn this?
What other payoff do you get when you are doing this?
What strengths, skills or talents are you using when you do this?
You mentioned X, Y and Z just now. How are those things connected to your work here at Scriber?

Asking and responding to these questions with each other helped us understand how students might feel when we use the 17 Questions skillfully. From our work with *Your Future Now*, we had already embraced the following truths:

- Students want to be successful, i.e., to feel competent, confident and connected.
- Students want to have their voices heard and be able to contribute to something beyond themselves.
- Students want to have high expectations for themselves.
- Students have strengths, skills, and talents that they may be unaware of.
- Part of our role as educators is to help students become more than they ever thought possible.

These truths apply to us as well, and the Question Club helped us get there. After experiencing the deeper connections we felt, we wondered what would happen if we had more of these conversations with students. We agreed that the feeling of connectedness would increase for our entire school.

STAFF REFLECTIONS:

Liza Behrendt, Leadership and Entry

Question Club has made all the difference for me. I don't think I'd have grown any real confidence without it. Prior to our meetings, it felt awkward to practice the 17 Questions. I would do it—I have them posted right next to my desk and referred to them regularly. I just felt like I was trying on someone else's coat.

I'm still no expert. I feel awkward at times and am not sure which question to use in a given situation. Yet the concepts and techniques are beginning to feel more natural and accessible in the moment. I learned a lot from practicing with staff members (and while interviewing a student with Cal next to me) about how and when to go deeper, how and when to ask a student to expand on something, and what success looks and feels like.

By becoming more comfortable with and adept at asking students these questions, I have been able to embody and convey the understanding that students are in charge of their own lives. For me this is the most essential piece of all of *Your Future Now*: students transforming in ways such that they begin taking charge of their lives and gaining support as they do so.

Dave Zwaschka, English

Practicing the questions has been extremely helpful; in fact, as we've used them with each other during Question Club, I've found myself challenged to really listen to my colleagues, to think hard about which follow-up or extending question to ask. We often interview each other in triads, allowing one person to be the meta-participant and reflect back to the interviewer how he/she heard the conversation go, noting its direction and asking probing questions regarding decisions the interviewer made.

These "mock interviews" don't seem "mock" when we're having them. Although we all know we're practicing to some degree, the questions have led to fascinating conversations and a strengthening of staff bonds. They are just as effective in building relationship between colleagues as they are in building relationships between staff and students. I look forward to our Question Club for a variety of reasons. Of course applying the questioning techniques helps in my work with students, but just as important is the opportunity to get to know my friends on staff in a deeper way.

Marjie Bowker, English

Question Club has been a highlight for me this year; it's amazing that I learned more about some of my colleagues during ten minutes of active listening than I have in the entire eight years I've worked with them.

One day at lunch—weeks before our first Question Club—some of us were talking about how badly our days were going. This evolved into what we humorously referred to as a "Bad Teacher Anonymous" meeting. We took turns stating, "My name is _____, and I am a bad teacher because…" We all laughed, but most of us commented later how much relief we felt in just being honest about our experiences. We share a very difficult job with many daily pressures and endless potential to learn from our mistakes.

Question Club accomplished the same effect. These meetings allowed us to share, express, listen and deepen our relationships while improving our ability to ask good questions in Appreciative Inquiry style.

Leighanne Law, Library and English:

I finally understand what we've been talking about all of this time. While it was happening, I was able to watch the decisions Peter made (during our triad practice) and analyze why he chose the questions he did and to think about which ones I might ask. It was a more hands-on way to practice than just to read scripts of how discussions have worked with other teachers and students. I was more confident today as I used the questions with students.

It was also a really cool way to get to know each other and I feel this practice is making us a stronger staff. Questions Club made the questions ours instead of Cal's, and the feedback I received from others helped me put into words what I hadn't given thought to.

Peter Folta, Social Studies

Question Club has been very helpful. I now understand how the questions might feel as the person being asked. It was good practice, especially to watch someone else try it. I felt a breakthrough after the first time we held club and actually spoke with one of my students about graduation the next day using some of the techniques because they were fresh in my mind. It takes time to make the paradigm shift and to retrain yourself to approach students in this way.

John King, Director of Education, Health and Leadership, Southern Oregon University

Having a forum to respond to these questions could have something of a therapeutic effect and help teachers refocus on their core qualities and commitments. We've found that effect in other similar research projects: reconnecting with these type of questions acts as a catalyst for animating and sustaining more intentional practice.

Ideally, the Question Club can be a tool that facilitates building more meaningful networks and communities of practice. Collecting and analyzing teachers' responses could help identify and connect teachers in different schools who are struggling with similar issues or aspiring to similar goals. That would be hugely beneficial in terms of supporting intentional practice.

From the perspective of those of us working to provide material support to teachers, educator communities engaging in practices like the Question Club could also help unearth ideas about what types of support are helpful. A lot of so-called "professional development" initiatives miss the mark because they address issues of concern to administrators rather than teachers. So, here's an opportunity to work from the ground up and hear directly from teachers about their authentic concerns, needs and hopes.

Chapter Nine
THE ROAD TO SUCCESS
Offering Clear Communication

Some schools call it "homeroom," but at Scriber we call it "Family." Each teacher is assigned between 15-20 students and is charged with building relationships, holding student/parent/teacher conferences (we call them SLP's—Student Learning Plans), and generally tracking these students until they graduate. If one of our Family members is falling behind, we often call "wrap-around" meetings and include students, teachers, counselors and parents in our discussions. We have 15-minute "Family" classes to begin the day and we also have Sustained Silent Reading (SSR) together after lunch for 20 minutes.

Every family class is run differently, but our main goal is to build connections. When we began to envision futures with our students and to help them identify their strengths, skills and talents, we knew that a lot of this work needed support at the Family level.

An ongoing frustration for many of us was keeping track of credits. During SLP meetings, we would look at Skyward, our district's computerized student record system, together and try to decode which credits had been earned and which were lacking. At a school where credit retrieval is so prevalent, this was a nightmare; we couldn't remember and neither could the student. Sometimes a student would meet with a counselor and go over graduation plans and then forget everything once they left the office. We needed a better tracking system.

When Cal was approached with an idea regarding how to track credits in a fun, colorful way that included stickers, he gave us the green light to develop what we now call our "Road to Success" poster. We sought an artist, Rebecca Jones, who had been connected to our school for career days, and she agreed to make some mock-ups for us. (Contact Rebecca Jones, hello@rebjones.com to create an individualized poster for your school.)

How to decode the Road to Success poster:

Each circle represents one quarter credit, totaling 88 quarter credits, and each subject is separated by the number of credits required. Educational Milestones (tests necessary to pass for graduation) are on the periphery. Stickers are placed within the circles to signify each credit earned or milestone reached.

Names go in the blank space in the middle of the bottom circle, and, most importantly, we ask students to write their future goals in the blank space in the middle of the top circle. Many say, "But I'm not sure what I want to do yet," to which we reply, "That's OK. There's room to list a lot of careers as you change your mind." It's interesting to witness the progression of some students' goals in this way.

Many teachers display these posters in their classrooms—as long as it's OK with the students—and some keep them in a special place and only pull them out during SLP meetings. Many of us begin our conferences by asking, "Has anything changed about your future goal?" and this begins our heart and soul discussion.

Both students and parents are invited to place the stickers on the corresponding circles. Almost every time we hear comments like, "This is the first time I have understood graduation requirements."

> *The Road to Success poster is helpful to me because I can see my progress in a different way other than just numbers.*
> *— Bruno, student*

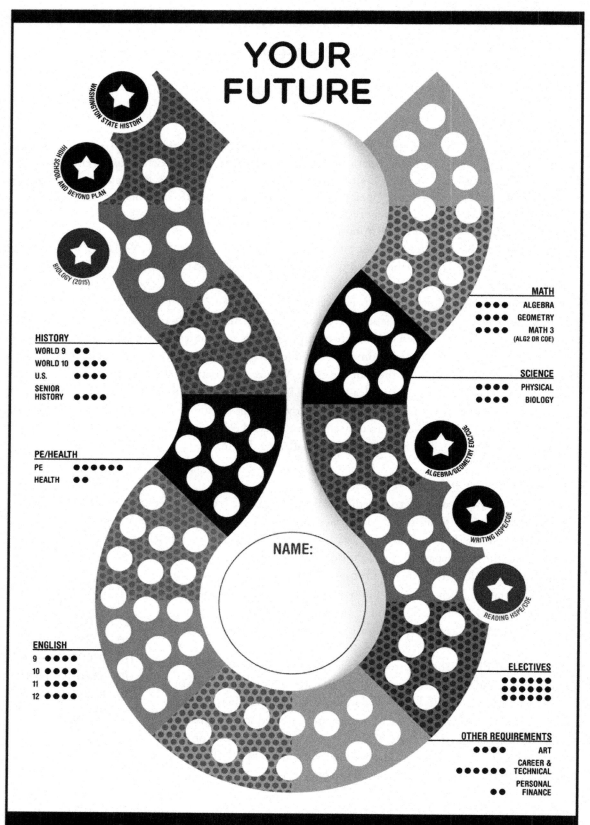

YOUR FUTURE

WASHINGTON STATE HISTORY

HIGH SCHOOL AND BEYOND PLAN

BIOLOGY (2015)

MATH
- • • • • ALGEBRA
- • • • • GEOMETRY
- • • • • MATH 3
  (ALG2 OR COE)

SCIENCE
- • • • • PHYSICAL
- • • • • BIOLOGY

ALGEBRA/GEOMETRY EOC/COE

WRITING HSPE/COE

READING HSPE/COE

HISTORY
- WORLD 9 • •
- WORLD 10 • • • •
- U.S. • • • •
- SENIOR HISTORY • • • •

PE/HEALTH
- PE • • • • • •
- HEALTH • •

ENGLISH
- 9 • • • •
- 10 • • • •
- 11 • • • •
- 12 • • • •

NAME:

ELECTIVES
- • • • • • •
- • • • • • •
- • • • • • •

OTHER REQUIREMENTS
- • • • • ART
- • • • • • • CAREER & TECHNICAL
- • • PERSONAL FINANCE

SLHS ROAD TO SUCCESS

REFLECTIONS

Mike Carey, Math

All of my students spend time updating their progress towards graduation during conferences. They are given a printout of all their credits and a batch of fun stickers to apply to their personal poster. They find immediate satisfaction in scoring all the credits they have "in the bank." Credit awareness is power.

On a bigger level, the poster helps students figure out how many credits they have earned versus the total needed for graduation and they begin to appreciate how many years of high school they have completed. We talk about the fact that students can earn up to seven credits per year at Scriber, so no matter how many credits they are behind, they can catch up by working hard.

One student I helped thought he had earned 15 out of 22 credits and he considered himself a junior. When we sat down and made his poster, he realized he had only earned 11 credits. This realization was frustrating at first, but soon his future plan crystallized. He clearly understood he was halfway done and needed to attend high school for two more years to collect his credits.

Dave Zwaschka, English

I asked one of my Family students, "How did you feel our conference went last week?"

"I think it went really well," he answered.

"Could you elaborate a bit more?"

"Sure. My Road to Success chart showed which requirements I need to graduate. I have a lot of history credits to earn, still, but then we talked about the two history CBL's I have almost completed I realized that I'm closer in that area than I thought."

"What would it mean for you to earn these credits?" I asked.

"It would mean I'm a half-credit closer to graduation," he said. "It would mean a lot."

He hadn't worked on either of these CBLs since the fall, but after talking about them, he became very interested in finding them and completing the relatively small amount of work still required. He came in today with both packets.

Deb Walters, Counselor

Since the inception of our work with the *Your Future Now* grant, I have reaped the benefits of having more of the staff speaking our "counseling center foreign language." The conversations Family teachers are having with the Road to Success posters mirror the conversations I have every day with students and parents. More students now understand that graduation does not simply hinge on the amount of credit earned but includes achievement of the educational milestones as well.

With more of us having conversations with students about their futures, we are building more awareness. Our students know that we care and certainly expect that we will all be asking them about their plans.

> When I first heard about credits I just brushed it off because I couldn't understand or see what a credit was. When I was told I had 17 credits left, I was like, "OK, cool, what does that mean?" Now that we have the posters, it's like playing a video game and your experience points are filling up. You can see how far you have to go to meet your goal.
> —Mitch, student

Marjie Bowker, English

The Road to Success poster has alleviated a lot of anxiety for me. Whenever I had to discuss credits with one of my Family members, all of the numbers on the printout swam in front of me and I couldn't make sense out of it for myself, let alone for my students. Because I am a visual learner, the colors and stickers have saved me (and them). Every student in my Family class now knows where he/she is on the path to graduation.

I now begin all of my conferences by asking if anything has changed for the goal listed in the top middle of the poster; I enjoy listing new dreams under previous ones and the question always fosters great discussion.

One example:

At the beginning of the year, one of my students had written "Automotive Technician" as his future career goal on his poster. He loves cars and thinks about them all the time—often to the exclusion of other things (like class work). He had struggled with math and a few other classes and would finish ninth grade lacking credits.

At his conference, I asked, "Has anything changed regarding this career goal?"

"Yes," he answered. "Give me a pen."

I did, and he wrote "Automotive Business Owner."

"Interesting!" I said. **"How did you decide that?"**

"Well, I don't want to just be someone's handyman. I want to own a shop so that I can not only work on cars, but so that I can collect them and sponsor people for competitions, you know, for drifting."

"That sounds great," I said. "Because you love cars and you love to make your own rules."

He laughed. "Yep."

For the rest of our conference, we talked about his classes and how he was doing in light of his goal.

"Now that you know where you're headed, it seems that math will have more importance for you," I said.

"Yeah, because I need to be good at all of that stuff. I need to know everything to be a good businessman. I have to know math, history, English…"

"Yes, that's right," I agreed.

Kristi Myers, Learning Support Teacher

The Road to Success poster has helped students gain a realistic picture of what it takes to graduate. So often a sheet full of columns and numbers is very confusing to students who don't think in spreadsheets. This visual organizer has made explaining the complicated relationship between graduation and credits earned extremely powerful. Students take pride in each sticker they place on their road and ask to meet so they can see the progress.

Andrea Hillman, Associate Principal

On one wall in every teacher's classroom, you see these Road to Success posters—they mean something here. Students refer to them, teachers refer to them, and during conferences they provide a touchstone and visual check-in for students to be able to articulate what they are doing (and in some cases what they have not been doing) to their parents, their Family teachers and themselves. It is another example of a living document that provides meaningful guidance on a daily basis for staff and students.

Trinity Meriwood, Business Education and Graphic Arts

The poster is great for students and parents who are visual learners. It is a great reality check for students that are (or believe they are) nearing graduation.

Coley Armstrong, Entry and Social Studies

The new Entry students are excited to complete their Road to Success posters. They all feel that the posters can help them determine how much high school they have left and whether or not their career choice is in line with their academic goals.

Richard Yi, Math

Since I'm still fairly new to Scriber, the Road to Success poster has helped me to get to know more about my Family students in terms of their interests and future goals. I've also gotten to know how many credits they've earned so far and how many more they need to earn to graduate. Some of my students (unfortunately, not all) took joy in placing stickers on their posters to signify how much they've achieved so far during conferences.

Peter Folta, Social Studies

The Road to Success poster has helped substantially in conferences, especially when a student is a junior or senior. In particular this is the case when they can explain it to a parent or guardian; it sparks a conversation about what it takes to graduate. Filling in the future dream or occupation is also an action that gets students and parents talking. In some cases I am left out of this conversation; I get to be the observer. It's amazing what parents learn about their kids in conferences.

> *The poster helps me visualize where I am with my credits and helps me think about the future.*
> —Aaron, student

Chapter Ten
CLASSES DESIGNED WITH SUCCESS IN MIND

Steps to Success (S2S) and Leadership

by Liza Behrendt

Two classes at Scriber specifically arose from our *Your Future Now* work. Steps to Success (S2S) is a class that every student in the school takes for an hour per week all year long; leadership class is offered as an elective. This chapter introduces each of these classes and illuminates the aspects that are interwoven with *Your Future Now*.

Steps to Success: The Need for Grounding

Early on in our work with *Your Future Now*, a goal was identified: any staff member should be able to stop any student in the hallway, ask the student what his or her plan was for after high school, and receive a response that was well thought out and that reflected an achievable vision.

This was beginning to happen. Some students were able to articulate their dreams for the future. Some could list their interests, strengths, skills, and talents, and some could even express an understanding of how high school studies related to the overall picture. Through motivational interviewing we were fostering the culture we aimed to create.

We began to recognize, however, that many students did not know who or where they were within this framing. Some students' dreams were scant, perfunctory, or disconnected from what their own passions seemed to indicate. Some were not in touch with their interests and abilities, and some did not know how to access helpful resources.

For decades, the staff of Scriber has been devoted to student success. The Entry program for students coming to Scriber has historically centered on three questions: "Who am I? Where am I going? What do I have to declare?" which invites students to explore their strengths, skills and talents. For years, our career specialist has connected students with scholarships, training programs and college application processes—including financial aid, job preparation (such as how to prepare for an interview), and so on. All of these staff members have been powerful in their abilities.

Even so, there did not seem to be a place for comprehensive incubation of students' dreams. Somewhere during the second year of *Your Future Now*, a subcommittee called "Future Ops" realized Scriber needed to provide students with more grounding for their dreams; we wanted to make sure no student slipped through the cracks. To fulfill our mission—to ensure that *all* students become successful by helping them identify, develop, and maximize their strengths, skills, and talents—we needed to address these gaps and disconnects in our approach. More students needed more information more consistently. From this place, "Steps to Success" or "S2S" was born.

The Birth of Steps to Success (S2S)

Scriber students came up with the name "Steps to Success." Beginning in the third year of our work, we modified the academic schedule to include S2S, a weekly, one-hour class that all students take all school year. The class

> I liked the dream board because it made me think about what I want to do when I get older. Teachers at my previous high school always bugged me about graduating and passing my classes but they never asked me what I wanted to do when I grew up and what I needed to do to get there.
> —Student

meets at the same time each week, and Family (homeroom) teachers work with their Family students.

In S2S students build confidence and expand competence around their own strengths, goals, skills, decision processes, interests, lifestyle plans, talents, career and college paths, learning styles and education plans. These aims, represented in the diagram below, were identified over the course of a year under the leadership of school counselor Lynn Willman, in collaboration with the Future Ops subcommittee.

Steps to Success (S2S) Aims

In the diagram below, the center box shows the most important elements included as part of each student's S2S plan. The four outer boxes contain the topics and aims we established as the highest priorities as we help students develop their plans.

Life Goals, Dreams & Plans

➤ Career Options & Exploration
➤ Dreams Exploration/Personal Goals
➤ College Options & Search Process
➤ One-year plan, two-year plan, five-year plan
➤ Lifestyle; Aspirations

Strengths, Skills, Talents & Interest (Self-Knowledge)

➤ Identify Talents & Passions
➤ Interest Inventories
➤ Learning Styles Inventory
➤ Strengths Assessments/ Inventories
➤ Strength Building

Your Steps to Success Plan

Who Am I? Where Am I Going? What Do I Have to Declare?

Strengths	Goals
Skills	Decision "Reflection"
Interests	Lifestyle Plan
Talents	Career Plan
Learning Style	Education Plan

What Do I Need/How Am I Going to Get There?

How Things Work

➤ Graduation Requirements
➤ College Entrance Requirements
➤ Educational Requirements for Career Interest Area
➤ Financing My Future Plan

Success Skills

➤ Career Readiness Skills
➤ College Readiness Skills
➤ Goal-Setting
➤ Decision-Making
➤ Communication & Interpersonal Relationship Skills
➤ Self-Advocacy Skills

We also developed a general sequence to be carried out throughout the school year, as shown below.

Steps to Success (S2S) Sequence

1. Start with passions and inventories
   a. Identify Talents and Passions
   b. Learning Styles Inventories
   c. Interest Inventories
2. Dreams Exploration/Personal Goals
3. Strength Assessments/Inventories
4. Strength Building
5. Goal-Setting—Personal Accountability
   a. One-year plan
   b. Two-year plan
6. Decision-Making—Personal Responsibility
7. Self-Advocacy Skills
8. Graduation Requirements
9. Career Options & Exploration
10. Career and College Readiness Skills
    a. 1st Semester Emphasis on Career
       i. Career Fair preparation
       ii. 5-year plan
       iii. Educational Requirements for Career Interest Area
       iv. Financing My Future—primarily counselors and career center
    b. 2nd Semester Emphasis on College
       i. College Fair preparation
       ii. 5-year plan
       iii. College Entrance Requirements
       iv. College Options & Search Process
       v. Financing My Future—primarily counselors and career center
    c. Both Semesters—Test Preparation
       i. 1st Semester—PSAT
       ii. 2nd Semester—SBA, ELA, HSPE, EOC
11. Communication & Interpersonal Relationship Skills

S2S Curriculum Development and Activities

Our staff develops the S2S curriculum collaboratively. After much consideration, Future Ops and the whole staff decided not to adopt a third-party curriculum, primarily because the right curriculum did not exist. We realized that our mission statement needed to be supported in a more tailored way, using bits and pieces of existing curricula. Collaborative curriculum development is not easy, yet we wanted to capture the best thinking and skills of all staff members and to share the sense of ownership and accomplishment. Periodically we determine the S2S activity plan several weeks ahead, with different staff members taking responsibility for designing and providing all resources needed for learning plans on different topics.

A sense of our S2S activities may be found by glancing through the list of activity titles below. Each activity is associated with one of the theme areas that are shown in the S2S aims above.

S2S Activities

Dream Boards

Finding Your Place

Goals Pyramid

True Colors

Pumpkin Carving Day

Welcome New Students

Veteran's Day Awareness

WOIS Interest Inventory

Holiday Family Day

Scriber Strengths Posters

Kindness Videos

Gratitude Cards

Defining You: Branding and Strengths

Lifetime Achievement Award

Preparing for Futures Fair

Futures Fair Event

Student Recognition Assembly

Student Evaluation of S2S

Mind Map Your Dreams and Skills

"Wing Ding" Social Events by School Area

Scriber March Madness Goal Setting

Mindfulness and Stress Management

Earth Day

Test Taking and Resiliency

Goal Setting

Hands-on and Outdoor Games by Teams

Study Hall

Check-in with S2S Teacher

Senior Honor Day

Selected S2S Lesson Plans

Here are a few of the S2S activities with learning plans. These were selected as some of the favorites by both staff and students.

Dream Boards—Designed by Marjie Bowker and Liza Behrendt
(Two Class Periods)

What are we doing?

Each student will design a "Dream Board" filled with words and images which reflect his/her dreams, goals and intentions for the future.

Why are we doing this?

Dreams provide students with a reason to be at school; those who have dreams don't drop out. We want to ask students what their dreams are—not only to establish a connection, but so we can help them on their road to success.

(Direct students' attention to our mission statement before beginning this activity.)

Materials needed to begin:

- quality magazines—National Geographic, sports, science, outdoor, artistic and home magazines
- scissors and glue sticks for each student
- large card stock paper for each student

Procedures:

1. Lead a brainstorming activity to help students identify their dreams, goals and intentions for the future. Possible prompts (read aloud to your class, slowly and with pauses):
   Close your eyes for a minute, or have a soft gaze toward the floor, and think about the following questions...
   - What makes you really happy?
   - If you could do ANYTHING with your life, what would it be?

- Imagine yourself about five years in the future in a job you love which pays well enough for you to enjoy life outside of work. What is the most interesting thing you can visualize? Is there a way you can get paid to do that?
- When you are old enough to be a grandparent–whether you actually become one or not–what do you want to be able to tell young people about life and what you did with yours?
- As you are imagining your ideal job, notice the following: Are you working with other people or by yourself? Are you wearing comfortable clothes or are you in a suit (or a comfortable suit)? Are you active, sitting at a desk, or a little bit of both? Imagine yourself feeling satisfied with this work at the end of the day.
- Take a moment and think about specific goals you have for this year. What is going to make you feel really proud when you look back on everything in June?

2. Discuss as a class.
3. When your class is ready, make the magazines available. Invite students to cut out all words and images that resonate with them. They don't have to use all of them, but it's important that they have a good collection in order to proceed to the next step.
4. When students have a pile of images and words, invite them to arrange them and glue them down on the board in a way that best expresses who they are.
5. (optional) Ask students to make a list of words that represent the pictures on the board. Using these words, have them write a statement about their future dreams, goals and intentions.
6. Share posters with each other.

Defining You—Designed by Zach Taylor, Career and College Specialist

Purpose: To think about your individual strengths and how to capitalize on them to create your dream future. These strengths can be used with friends and acquaintances, at school and with future employers.

1. What Brands Say to You (15 min)
   a. Take five minutes to identify as many brands as you can in class at this moment (clothing, objects, etc).
   b. Talk about what these brands mean or say about the product and/or the people who use them.
   c. Offer examples of other famous brands (Starbucks, Michael Jordan, Apple, etc.) and do the same thing.
   d. What do you feel just by seeing each of those symbols/brands?

2. What Is a Personal Brand? (5 min)
   a. A personal brand: it's not just your personal assets, but it's what you want to be known for.
   b. It's what makes you unique.
   c. It's what people remember you for.
   d. It's what keeps people loyal to you
   e. Before you leave for lunch, think of some people that have famous brands.
      i. Michael Jordan
      ii. Steve Jobs
      iii. The Kardashians
      iv. Dr. Dre
   f. List 2-5 words that define each of them.

3. Defining YOU (15 min)
   a. Spend time thinking of the answers to these questions. (10 min)
      i. What are some words you use to describe yourself?
      ii. What qualities do you have that keeps others loyal to you?
      iii. Think of three words that describe the lasting impression you want to leave with others after they meet you.
      iv. What are three things you do well?
      v. How will you make an impact with these capabilities?
   b. Take a few moments and think about what comes to the surface as the common themes in the answers to these questions.
   c. What 2-5 words capture those themes? (2 min)
   d. Compose a brief paragraph that includes those 2-5 words, what you do well, and how you will make an impact with these capabilities. (3 min)
   e. This paragraph is what your brand is all about

4. Your Brand
   a. Create some sort of logo or image that is representative of your brand
      i. Draw
      ii. Words/graphics

Scriber Strength Posters—Designed by the Leadership Class Students

Part I		Part II
"Talk About Scriber" Prompts *What students like about Scriber and how to make Scriber even better.*		Poster Themes *Describe what Scriber is about and how we can make it even better.*
IDEA: Have a facilitator (can be a student) ask students to each contribute an idea about something that makes them feel good, a word or an action. Can be focused on school and what happens here. Prompt with questions: 1. What do you like/love about Scriber? (Can also ask what you don't like, to help get that addressed.) 2. How could you make Scriber a better place? 3. What can the leadership class do to make Scriber a better place? 4. What can teachers do to make Scriber a better place? 5. What can you (students) do to make Scriber a better place?		1. Write what you would like to read, what would make you feel better. Example: This world needs you," or "You're beautiful." 2. Continue the "You make a difference when..." 3. Quotes by or about famous people such as Helen Keller ("The best and most beautiful things in the world cannot be seen or even touched—they must be felt with the heart."), MLK, Rosa Parks, etc. 4. Simply put artwork on posters and put them out there—basically to have more images of beauty or interest. 5. Put quotes WITH images! Make sure this is about what the students think and want—let the students take as much initiative and leadership as possible.

S2S Progress Notes

S2S is a work in progress. In March of our first year we conducted staff and student surveys, asking questions in Appreciative Inquiry style, such as "What is good about S2S?" and "How can S2S be made even better?" While we received our share of nonplussed or negative responses, positive and constructive comments ruled the day. As of this writing, we are deep in the throes of working out plans for the coming school year, hopeful that we can build on our successes to evolve the program.

We understand from students' survey responses that we need to make S2S more lively and fun by including more games, art projects, hands-on tasks, food, group activities and discussions. We understand from teachers and other staff members that curriculum development takes time, as does working from a lesson plan that someone else has developed. We found significant value in S2S activities, yet recognize that there is room to grow as we develop this program.

> *My favorite S2S activity was the goal pyramid because it helped us think about what we are going to do when we get to the age of having to take care of ourselves and our family. Knowing where you're going in life is very important, whether you think it is or not.*
> *—Student*

Leadership Class

Michele Rupe, leadership class teacher at GATES High School in Tacoma, Washington knocked the socks off of Scriber's Marjie Bowker at the Washington Association for Learning Alternatives annual conference in 2012. Eventually, Marjie arranged a visit to observe what was happening there.

The Scriber visitors—three students and a fellow teacher, Peter Folta—were extremely impressed with what they witnessed. Highlights included a learning environment that shares many foundational values with *Your Future Now*. For example, educators at GATES teach "appropriate school behaviors rather than punish" by building trusting relationships, (see gates.fpschools.org). Michele's leadership class also emphasizes multiple programs for recognizing student successes. Upon return to Scriber, Marjie, Peter and the students decided that Scriber needed a leadership class, too.

Now back up to 1972 when the original TV show "Zoom" hit the scene, featuring teens and tweens engaged in exciting, grown-up projects. As a child I was positively impacted by the zest and empowerment of these young people, and held that vision for, ahem, many years. Through subsequent study of transformative learning, many experimental projects and with inspiration from Paulo Freire, Joseph Beuys, Malala Yousafzai, and the New Leaf Leadership Academy in Martinez, California, I was thrilled to become Scriber's leadership teacher. For decades I had wanted to facilitate leadership in high school.

The funny part of this role has been that I rarely "teach" in the traditional sense. The class is designed around multiple concepts that place the students in the driver's seat: democratic education, project-based learning, place-based learning, experiential learning, and transformative learning, where meaning making through reflection is paramount. Students consider project requests by staff and also brainstorm their own possibilities. As a group, they then select projects they are most passionate about.

In our first year, students designed and executed projects such as Spirit Week and a spirit assembly, which are not common in our school. They designed welcoming activities and made posters for new Entry students. They organized a food drive for local food banks in partnership with a local leader, and a fundraiser for cancer research and peace initiatives in the Middle East. The culminating project selected by student three quarters in a row involved giving donated clothing and other items directly to people in Seattle who

> *My confidence went from thought to action.*
> *—Student*

are homeless (note that a significant portion of the students in the class have been homeless themselves). Students also present "teaching topics," combining research into their skills, strengths, talents and dreams for the future and weaving in themes related to leadership.

Your Future Now and Leadership

The *Your Future Now* tenets (discussed in Chapter One) show up every day in the leadership class. As students take charge of the class activities, they are actually practicing taking charge of their own lives and futures. They transform from receptive to active learners and shape their own learning on an ongoing basis.

Students create mastery experiences through the many projects, which leads to enhanced belief among students in their own capabilities (self-efficacy). We frame the "failures" that occasionally come along as excellent learning events, letting experience and reflection be the main teachers. Since the students select the projects, they are highly motivated and engaged, and they regularly develop their own strategies for overcoming obstacles and rebounding from setbacks (resiliency). By framing our project selection process as an opportunity to make our world better, we align with Appreciative Inquiry. By allowing students to grapple as a group with habitual ambivalence, come to a place of readiness to choose projects, and then design and execute project plans, we embody the intentions of motivational interviewing.

> I have learned that being a leader isn't something you only do in a class, but throughout your lifetime.
> —Student

> We need to create trust in the classroom so students feel comfortable sharing their hopes and dreams.
> —Zachary Taylor, Career and College Specialist

> My favorite S2S activity was "True Colors" because it showed me a lot about myself and others. It made us as a school come together a little more.
> —Student

> All of the activities offered us the opportunity to think about the future in concrete, tangible ways, and get to know each other better in the process.
> —Dave Zwaschka, Teacher

> What would make me happy would be if I could help the community in some way — for example, the homeless. I would also like to make an impact at Scriber. I want students to know that the leadership class is here to help the school.
> —Student

> You have to just put your fear and anxiety of messing up to the side and focus on the goal.
> —Student

> The activities that my students most enjoyed and learned from were the ones in which there was some movement, some reflection and some discussion.
> —Leighanne Law, Teacher

Chapter Eleven

THE SCRIBER LAKE WRITING PROGRAM
AND
YOUR FUTURE NOW

by Marjie Bowker

The year before Cal came to Scriber suggesting the importance of asking students about their dreams, goals and plans for their futures, local author Ingrid Ricks and I stumbled upon the transformative power in asking students to write about their pasts.

When I learned it wasn't until Ingrid gave herself permission to write *Hippie Boy, A Girl's Story* and share it with others that she was able to let go of the pain from her childhood, I knew my students deserved that same opportunity.

We quickly discovered our shared passion for exploring the inherent power in personal storytelling. Ingrid started coming into my English classes to discuss *Hippie Boy* and to ask one question: "What's *your* story?" And despite the issues that were constantly interfering with their ability to focus— homelessness, poverty, abuse and drug and/or alcohol issues—my students were eager to write raw, honest responses to that question. They were leaving their hearts and souls on paper, blowing everyone away with their courage. By the end of that year we had published our first student collection of stories, *We Are Absolutely Not Okay*.

The rush of excitement—and the complete buy-in from students—was mixed with some worry as well. Was I doing right by my students in encouraging them to set detailed, painful truths out for the world to read? We were working in conjunction with our counseling staff and our school psychologist was adamant that exposing truths was healthy. We made every effort to ensure that each step was student-directed with a lot of adult counsel. But still, I had a lot of questions.

Therefore, when Cal came to Scriber that next fall, every word of his philosophy resonated with me. Not only did I learn that research supported our efforts, but I realized our writing program was a practical implementation of *Your Future Now*.

In the following pages, I have broken down how the *Your Future Now* elements of self-efficacy and resiliency tie to the Scriber Lake Writing Program. First, for a better understanding of how our writing/publishing process works at Scriber, I will define the four steps involved:

1. We begin with a narrative writing unit in my English classes. All students write three-to-five page scenes from their lives according to the Common Core State Standards for Narrative Writing. A minimum of two drafts is required, but many exceed this requirement.
2. All students are given the opportunity to share their scenes during a class reading at the end of the unit. We turn off the lights, light a lamp as a spotlight, and readers sit on a stool in front of the class.
3. Students interested in publishing their stories can take our spring publishing mini-course, a week-long, very intense course in which we edit our stories (endlessly), come up with a theme, cover and bios and publish a book. (We hold weeklong mini-courses twice per year: one in the fall and one in the spring. All teachers choose the subject matter for their mini-courses.)
4. Published writers are given many opportunities to read their stories in school and community settings.

SELF-EFFICACY: STUDENTS' BELIEF IN THEIR CAPACITY TO PERFORM

Student belief in self is the biggest indicator of success. The following points are tied to increasing self-efficacy within our program.

More than ever, I realize that when students say something is "stupid" or refuse to do class work, it's either because they don't find the work meaningful or because many years of "failure" have stripped them of all confidence in their abilities. The following elements increase students' desire for learning as well as their own belief that they can learn.

1. Building Self-Efficacy: Create Mastery Experiences

Over the years, I have developed narrative writing curriculum (*They Absolutely Want to Write: Teaching the Heart and Soul of Narrative Writing*) that breaks the writing process down into basic, tangible elements. Each small success during classroom practice builds confidence until students forget they "can't" write.

My mnemonic for the five elements of narrative writing is SCEDS (Setting, Character, Emotions, Dialogue and Sensory Details). The technique is to ask them to identify sensory details from projected pictures, then write themselves into the scenes using the words they have identified. Most students— especially struggling ones— respond well to visual cues and quickly engage with their emotions, which these lessons invite. When writing is made this easy, every single student participates. My motto is "Give them the words, then they will write."

After they have experienced success during practice sessions, they then transfer the skills gained when writing about their own experiences. All of these elements are part of the Common Core State Standards for Narrative Writing.

Josh Blair, 17
The SCEDS lessons put me more in touch with my senses.

Brieaunna Dacruz, 16
I am more of a picture person, so the visuals helped me get deeper into my past where I could grab the details.

Santino Dewyer, 17
Brainstorming the sensory details helped me describe things to my readers so they could have a picture in their heads.

2. Building Self-Efficacy: Create a Sense of Purpose

A sense of purpose is inherent in all steps of this writing process; however, below I have collected student responses from one of the first steps: the "What, Why, How?" discussion I held at the beginning of this year's narrative writing unit for my English 11-12 class (see Chapter Three). I addressed the whole class with each question and recorded their answers using a document camera to facilitate the discussion.

Q. What are we learning?

- We are writing a narrative scene from something that happened in our lives—something that impacted us and made us grow or change.
- We're learning the SCEDS elements: how to write Setting, Character, Emotion, Dialogue and Sensory Details into our scenes.

Q. Why are we learning this?

- So that we can get our stories out.
- So that we know we are not alone.

- Because everyone has a story and it's important to identify ours.
- Helps get the negative energy out.
- Helps us to communicate our experiences clearly.
- Helps us to get in touch with our senses.

Q. How will we use this knowledge now or in the future?

- We will understand people better—what motivates them.
- Will help us to be ourselves.
- We will know how to get into another person's shoes.
- To learn how to write descriptively is something that can be used in many professions: police work, law, business—anything, really. Oh, and if we want to be a writer!
- We can help other people write their stories.
- It might help us make better decisions about what we do or the choices we make because we have looked at it objectively.
- Helps us to look at our own experiences from an outside perspective.
- Makes things feel better.
- We can stand up for people with more confidence.

Reflection:

Because writing our stories and publishing them has become a part of our school culture, many of these students already had that in mind during this discussion, even though this is just the first step in the writing process: But it's always good to set the tone and an intention for why we do what we do.

3. Building Self-Efficacy: Expose Students to Role Models

The reason my students love Ingrid's book *Hippie Boy* so much is because they can see themselves in it; they understand the power struggle, the poverty and the strength it requires to grow up without ideal support from adults. The first day Ingrid comes into my classes, she talks about how unhealthy it was for her to hold the stress of her childhood in for so many years. She shares that getting her story out has allowed her to put the past in its place and move forward with a strong voice that has helped others.

This message resonates strongly with students. Not only do they realize that if Ingrid can tell her difficult story, they can too, but they are also motivated by the idea of helping others by helping themselves. Most students will say that knowing they aren't alone or hearing how someone else made it through a hardship has helped them to move forward with more confidence and provides them the ultimate purpose.

Vasiliy Karpinskiy, 14

After finishing Hippie Boy *I wondered, "What is the point of hiding something that makes you feel bad for years?" The way writing my story helped me: well, I definitely did lose a lot of stress and now that a few people know, they are helping me get over it.*

Michael Coffman, 14

Hippie Boy *inspired me to write my story because it's a true story written by someone who went through difficult situations. It was powerful to read through these events from Ingrid's point of view. Writing my story helped me let go of what happened and took away a lot of anger and resentment.*

Emmasariah Jensen, 14

Author of "Don't Cry, Princess" from *Behind Closed Doors: Stories from the Inside Out*

Reading Hippie Boy *helped me write my story because I read about how Ingrid went through things that I went through, too. Ingrid found her voice and her freedom. She proved that it wasn't easy, that sometimes everything just goes to hell. Knowing this, I was able to get my feelings out after holding them in my whole life.*

Aydan Dennis, 14

Writing my story helped me because it allowed me to release pent-up frustration without hurting others, and lifted a weight off my shoulders. It helped me to reveal other feelings I had about what I wrote, and helped me to realize that it's okay to share this story with others.

4. Building Self-Efficacy: Belief in the Person

I have many opportunities to express belief in students' abilities to write. My curriculum guide is titled *They Absolutely Want to Write* because, over and over again, I see students who previously had no confidence in their ability to express themselves become beautiful writers.

A few months ago a student told me he wanted to write a story, but wouldn't be able to because he "couldn't" write. So I "Cal Crowed" him.

"What made you decide that?" I asked.

"I've just always had a hard time getting things down on the page," he said.

"What if you could write? How would things be different?"

He paused for a moment, then said, "I would like that."

"What would it mean if I told you I believe you can write?"

He smiled in relief and said, "It would mean a lot. Like that maybe I really could do it."

He agreed to try, and, sure enough, became one of the most enthusiastic writers in his class; he even ended up publishing his story and never mentioned his "inability" again. I was surprised at how easily this transformation took place.

An even better situation is when students have these conversations with each other. I hear them saying, "Yeah, I didn't think I could do it, either. But I did it. You can, too."

RESILIENCY: THE ABILITY TO OVERCOME OBSTACLES AND REBOUND FROM SETBACKS

Resiliency is a cornerstone concept in *Your Future Now*. The following points illustrate how our program increases resiliency in students:

1. Resiliency: The Role of a Caring Adult

Many students have expressed that just sitting with the details of their painful experiences with an interested, caring adult has been "the best therapy." Being asked "How did you feel when she said that? What did the room smell like? What was hanging on the walls? What was your physical reaction to that emotion?" allows them to go back and re-experience the event, then gain an objective perspective on it. This kind of writing offers an excellent way to validate the pain of what happened, which is the ultimate form of listening. Now my students have a community of adults who know them and accept them for who they are. Just by putting the "What's your story?" question out there and being willing to listen to the answers without judgment, many opportunities are provided for adults to step in, show interest, and mentor these courageous students.

Brayan Hernandez, 17

Author of "One Shot" from *You've Got it All Wrong*

When I told my story for the first time, I felt like a can of soda being opened to release all of the fizz; all the negative energy that I had built over the years poured out and I lost the chains that were holding me back. Before, I was afraid to tell my story because of what everyone would think of me. But I found that instead of seeing me as a bad person, people saw me as someone who wanted to use his past to help other young people in similar situations.

Marika Evenson, 17

Author of "The Monster within Him" from *Behind Closed Doors: Stories from the Inside Out*

When Marjie gave us the assignment to write our stories in her English class, I cried. I just wanted to punch her. It's been very hard, but now I realize that through this writing experience, I have healed more than I ever could have imagined. I started out hating myself and now have come around to loving myself. Even though I hate what has happened to me in my life, it has made me who I am and I no longer want to change that. I don't think I would have ever felt that way fully without getting my story out. It has made me feel strong and has given me my power back.

Tattiyana Fernandez, 17

Author of "Replaced" from *You've Got it All Wrong*

Writing my story has been a huge achievement for me! It has helped me overcome so many of my problems, because until then I thought I was the only one who struggled with abandonment. Knowing that my deepest story can help someone is the best feeling in the world to me.

Tatam Walker, 16

Author of "Lil Red" from *Behind Closed Doors: Stories from the Inside Out*

It was really hard to write about Daunte's death because of the timing and the emotions involved. But once I saw it on paper, it felt good to get it out rather than wallowing in it. Writing didn't get me over his death, but it did help me handle it. I may even be using at this point if I hadn't written it; at the time I had thoughts of getting high to cover the pain and not to feel it anymore. It feels like a weight off my shoulders.

2. Resiliency: High Expectations

When students are confident in their abilities and their efforts are filled with meaning and purpose, they respond well to high expectations. I used to dread assigning papers; many of my students had never experienced success in writing and were not eager to fail again. But now, due to mastery experiences, the majority of my students excel in this unit and most turn in at least two drafts of a three-to-five page scene (typed and double-spaced). Those who decide to publish and take the spring mini-course often write multiple drafts to get every detail right. We expect their commitment, and they are happy to oblige. After all, what they are doing really matters to them.

My current goal is to transform my students into teachers of narrative writing. Three students did a trial run at Edmonds Community College class last fall as part of the college's adoption of *Behind Closed Doors* for their Community Read book for 2014-15. The students were so positive about their experience that I am now teaching a class called "Stories for Social Change." We are reading true stories of marginalized people, writing our own stories and learning how to teach each of the SCEDS (setting, character, emotion, dialogue, sensory details) elements so that we can mentor others.

My students are rising to the occasion and the energy is shifting to more student-directed endeavors for me to manage. To witness the transformation of students who have experienced so much failure has transformed my idea of what it means to be a teacher.

Maize Phillips, 17

Author of "Loser, Failure, Dumbass" from *Behind Closed Doors: Stories from the Inside Out*

The writing process was rough. I had over twenty drafts after working on my story for three months. But in the end it was worth it because writing and sharing my story has changed my perspective about other people.

Angel Seupmtewa, 18

Author of "Fly Away, Angel Baby" from *You've Got it All Wrong*

I wanted to write this story because I didn't want to keep it in any longer. After moving, Marjie and I emailed nine drafts of my story back and forth and it has helped me to come to terms with my past.

Shelby Asbury, 15
Author of "Good Intentions, Bad Results" from *Behind Closed Doors: Stories from the Inside Out*
The experience of teaching at the college was awesome. I mean, I'm 15 and people want me to teach them.

3. Resiliency: Giving Voice

Published writers in our program are given many opportunities to contribute. They read their stories in front of their peers, at other high schools, at local Rotary and Exchange Club Meetings, at local bookstores and conferences. We now have a partnership with Seattle Public Theater and each fall stories are adapted for the stage. Because our book was selected for Edmonds Community College's Community Read Program for 2014-15, instructors in many fields designed class curricula around one or more of the stories. As a result, we were invited to present at the college on multiple occasions and strengthened the relationship between our two campuses.

Students are empowered and validated with each contribution they make to their community and world; they now know that their voices are important.

In the fall of 2014, a tragic shooting occurred at a local high school. The next day, one of the writers messaged me, asking, "Do you think we could help students at that school write their stories? I feel like we could do it."

I was so moved by this gesture. Here was a student who had come full circle, from feeling like a failure to feeling like she had tools to contribute to someone else's healing in a tragic situation.

Maize Phillips, cont'd
It was awesome to speak of my story with a reporter from the Everett Herald and on the set of King 5 for the New Day Northwest show. I've been surprised to hear so many inspiring compliments about me being willing to share my story. We also had students from Eastmont High School in Wenatchee come to hear our stories and to learn about our writing program. A lot of them told me that they could relate to my struggles.

Tatam Walker, cont'd
Now that I've shared my story, many tell me about their own losses. They tell me 'I have felt what you felt.' That feels great, to get that support. It also feels good to be able to help others just through writing.

Marika Evenson, cont'd
We tell our stories hoping that they can help more than just us.

Destanee Stock, 17
Author of "One Kid's Lie" from *Behind Closed Doors: Stories from the Inside Out*
It feels good to share my story with others. I love knowing that I can make an impact and make other people happy. I like that.

WRITERS' REFLECTIONS

We invite students to reflect on their transformations to encourage high level thinking. We have done this in various forms, but in each case it's clear that the reflection solidifies and internalizes the experience to a deeper degree. Here are a few responses to a list of questions I gave to the *Behind Closed Doors* writers three months after publishing:

BRIEAUNNA DACRUZ

Author of "Closet Doors" from *Behind Closed Doors: Stories from the Inside Out*
What did you write your story about and why did you choose this subject?
I wrote about coming out to my parents because it was the biggest struggle of my life. I wanted to process it to let it go.

How have you changed since writing your story?

I'm a lot more open. I can now express things about myself with my family. Things have gotten easier because they understand me and what I went through better.

How does that feel?

It changed my life. It feels reassuring, like I can move forward and grow past it.

What was the writing process like for you?

It was very difficult. It brought back things I thought I forgot... unresolved conflicts. I had to face my emotions.

How does it feel to share your story with others?

It makes me feel good that I can help others through their own process of healing.

What responses have you gotten?

A lot of people have said "I'm sorry" because they didn't know what I was going through at the time. It's also been encouraging because people have never looked at me as a writer before. One student in a class I read my story to said, "I could live in your moment because of how you wrote it."

What might your life be like if you hadn't written this story?

I would have no sense of relief. I would still have weight on my shoulders. I wouldn't have the support I do now. I would be less understanding. I have opened up a lot.

SHELBY ASBURY

Author of "Good Intentions, Bad Results" from *Behind Closed Doors: Stories from the Inside Out*

What did you write your story about and why did you choose this subject?

I wrote about sexual abuse by an older man. I chose to write about this because it was a prominent thing in my life. It was weighing me down. I thought it would get better by writing about it.

How have you changed since writing your story?

I'm more mature. I'm more open with what happened. I'm more willing to help people, just knowing what a push did for me, how it helped me. I see people differently—I see them for what stories they might have. I don't judge people as fast as I used to. I didn't like being around people before. Now I'm OK if someone taps me on the shoulder. Before I was skittish.

What was the writing process like for you?

It sucked for the first couple of days. It put the pain back in my head and made me sad. Then it started to help me realize that it wasn't my fault and that I could move on. At the time it was happening I didn't know if I was a good person or not. But the writing helped me to see myself clearly.

How does it feel to share your story with others?

It was scary at first. I didn't want people to judge me. Now I feel a weight lifted off me every time I share it. I'm taking steps to becoming my own person. I'm getting stronger.

What kind of responses have you gotten?

"You're strong, you've got courage, I'm so happy you're still here." They tell me I've inspired them. They say, "Thank you for being strong enough to share this." It feels really good that my bad experience could be used for someone else's good.

What might your life be like if you hadn't written this story?

I would still be in bed crying every morning and night. I would still be scared to be around guys. I wouldn't trust people like I do now. Writing it made me see down a different path. Now I think, "Hey, maybe this person isn't so bad..."

MY STORY

Four years ago, I wanted to escape my teaching career. I felt that the gap between state requirements and what my students were dealing with outside of school was too large and that relevance was missing. I was constantly frustrated.

However, after watching student after student write about deep emotional pain and begin to take control of experiences that previously had control over them, I have changed. I have seen unimaginable traumas shared, accepted and taken in by groups of empathetic peers who then become passionate about sharing that release with others. I have watched former meth addicts, victims of abuse or neglect and children of extreme loss and trauma take leadership roles and encourage others to let go of their burdens through writing.

I now know that behind many struggling students is a father in prison, a mother's overdose or a cousin's death from driving under the influence. Knowing someone's story makes all the difference. When validation occurs and inherent resiliency is recognized and directed toward something meaningful, there is power. Struggling students respond in previously unimaginable ways—and they write. After they write, many move on to become more active learners who are planning for a better future.

Relevance used to be my biggest concern as a teacher. Now, however, I see my students viewing themselves as participants in a universal dialogue—participants who are making a difference in people's lives.

For more information about our program, please visit Scriber's web page under "About Us":
www.edmonds.wednet.edu/Page/12136

Chapter Twelve
STAFF TRANSFORMATIONS

While working toward the goal of student transformation, it's not surprising that many of us found ourselves transformed along the way. During our journey to bring students back into the center of their own education, we became more centered in our own teaching practice.

Although we never found the magic pill to cure poor attendance or to solve all of the issues that our population faces, our overall numbers rose dramatically in rates of enrollment and graduation. More students than ever before have a plan for the future and are seeking higher education. Most importantly, we like our culture better. We feel better—*way better*—about being at school every day, and look forward to how our efforts will continue to play out in our school's future.

With the intention of reflecting on our overall experience with this work, all staff members were invited to address the following questions:

How has our school transformed since implementing the *Your Future Now* vision?
How have you transformed as an educator?
If you are new(er) to this staff, what do you like about what you have seen so far?

Our reflections follow.

Paul Scott, Custodian

What I've seen in the short time I've been here: I've overheard some students talking to new students about what they need to do to graduate—a mentorship, if you will, that you just don't see that often anymore. A long time ago, I was on the verge of not graduating until some special teachers took me under their wing and put me back on the right path. I see that spirit still alive here. We may take a wrong turn once in a while, but that is life, and the path of life turns *a lot*!

I see staff really trying to reach out, using some great techniques to engage students in learning and to encourage them to reach for more. Each student is different, and I see staff continually trying to find that spark that is inside each of us, refusing to give up. I also see staff talking with each other and trying to find that spark in regards to different students and their styles of learning.

Lynn Willman, Counselor

In many ways, the *Your Future Now* project is a school counselor's dream come true; it is a model any school could implement. Because it is a school-wide effort, it has allowed us to increase the depth and richness of our student advising.

Our staff now shares a philosophy and a language; more importantly, we share a greater commitment to doing this work together and a responsibility for helping our students plan for their futures. It has changed us from a school where meaningful and caring conversations happen between some staff and some students some of the time, to a school where all teachers are regularly talking with all students about their futures, their hopes and dreams, and their strengths, skills and talents.

Our school's mission now reads *Scriber will ensure that all students becomes a success, by helping them identify, develop and maximize their strengths, skills and talents.* Isn't that what we are all about as educators, especially those of us who are school counselors? Isn't that why so many of us are drawn into and remain committed to this challenging profession?

We are here to help students fulfill their potential and see their unique gifts, even when they have not yet recognized them. We are here to help them experience success, to build upon their existing skills and to learn and discover new ones—to achieve their dreams.

Mike Carey, Math

I believe our school has transformed the way we communicate with our students, especially the disruptive ones.

Before, it was easy to fall into a confrontational posture when a student was agitated and acting out. My first thought used to be *How can I assert myself in this situation and control student behavior?* Since implementing the elements of *Your Future Now*, my response has softened because I realized that I do not want to control student behavior. My objective is to build strong interpersonal relationships with each student and learn about each one's passions and dreams. Instead of confronting a disruptive student, I now calmly and respectfully pose questions such as: How is your behavior helping your long term goal of completing high school? Going on to college? Getting a job in a field you really love?

Understanding the future hopes and dreams of our students gives us power to help them. I now counsel students by offering advice that addresses their personal goals.

Dave Zwaschka, English

Our *Your Future Now* work has challenged me to think about the relevance of my course, the relationships my students and I are building, and how the two are intertwined. Asking students *what* we're learning, *why* we're learning it and *how* they might use the information in the future has added depth and transparency to the work we're doing.

I like the focus on understanding the students' point of view and appreciating how many challenges the majority of them have overcome to simply be at school. Asking students to talk more about their lives—then listening closely—allows me to get to know them better and (I hope) invites them to reflect upon their own decisions and choices in a positive light.

I've enjoyed participating in what feels like a truly human approach to teaching and learning. The questions have given me more than just a larger repertoire of strategies; they have challenged me to listen deeply to what my students are saying, then respond with questions that invite them to see themselves as active agents of change in their own lives.

Michael Waldren, Science paraeducator

I arrived at Scriber recently, carrying an inaccurate understanding of what this school was about, yet am immensely satisfied with how my teaching journey has unfolded. I have been presented with a vast array of challenges and I can feel myself growing right alongside the students.

Typically, the students here have endured more adversity than most of their peers. The Write to Right program (Chapter Eleven) is an incredibly effective method of connecting to the students and the school. Many students have read their classmates' stories, which has made the camaraderie here palpable.

It has also been encouraging to observe that discussions between staff go beyond meetings and progress reports. The teachers and administrators are interested in more than just the school's graduation rate; the success and long term well-being of the student is also heavily taken into account. It has been a breath of fresh air to collaborate with my teaching peers and discuss how we can get students to succeed in their life goals rather than simply how to boost our reputation as a school.

Working at Scriber has been one of the best educational experiences I could have hoped for. It may be common in society to judge an alternative school as a step down educationally, but in my experience, I have never seen the proverbial arrow pointing as high as it is within this campus. The overall attitude is not how to get by and simply satisfy the standard, but how to establish dreams and never lose sight of them. That philosophy should unquestionably represent the educational ideology, and you will find it here at Scriber.

Fred Bonallo, School Resource Officer

I have worked at Scriber for eight years; I came here after 30 years in law enforcement. I like working in a school that focuses on helping students become successful members of our community and helping them achieve happy, productive lives. Our work with Cal's Center for Efficacy and Resiliency has equipped us with strategies to support our students' development. We do this by helping them identify and further develop their strengths, skills and talents.

The most important component of this work, in my opinion, is asking students to visualize a future for themselves they feel very passionate about, then communicating that vision to their classmates and teachers. This way, we know where they want to go and can help keep them on track when they stray. By speaking to students' hearts and souls—not just their heads—a more significant form of communication occurs that encourages more retention and relevance.

Not all students are ready for this type of relationship, but we have a very committed staff and processes in place to support them until they are more receptive. The teacher/student interpersonal relationships that I have observed as I move around the campus have made it clear that we are now developing better relationships; we have a better understanding of their needs. A lot of our past student contacts were punitive or confrontational, and this impeded progress and made classrooms uncomfortable for everyone. This was certainly job security for me, but poor for student and staff retention.

I look forward to continuing our work with the students at Scriber, celebrating our successes and learning from our mistakes.

Richard Yi, Math

By utilizing the 17 Questions with my students, I was able to learn more about their histories, family backgrounds, interests, strengths and weaknesses. Gaining information and knowledge about my students has helped me to teach concepts in a way that best fits their learning styles, rather than teaching the materials the same way to all of my students.

Trinity Meriwood, Business Education and Graphic Arts

My response is a bit of a hybrid because I was gone from teaching for two years and came from school environments that were very different (size of school, population demographics, etc).

One of the biggest differences I noticed immediately was Scriber's collaborative environment, from the beginning to the end of the day. Something that seems so small but makes a *huge* difference is that the majority of the teachers eat lunch together. This allows little things, like discussing student issues, to occur on a regular basis.

It has also changed me. I seek more opportunities to collaborate and to come up with ways for my graphic arts students to contribute for classroom needs or real world applications. For ten years I have felt very isolated and independent as an educator. Teaching marketing meant I was a department by myself and that my environments were not set up for easy collaboration. The large staff meant I would go to "all staff" meetings, look around the room, and see teachers I didn't recognize or had never spoken to. Once I got to Scriber, I was able to interact, collaborate and have discussions regarding student issues and successes; I have felt like a *part* of a school from the first day.

My students benefit in so many ways because of this that it's difficult to explain them all. Now I can give them design projects that are meaningful for the whole school—relevant and useful "real world" projects—not just fictional projects that I *think* might be useful.

Peter Folta, Social Studies

I feel like I've been armed with tools to help me better understand students and their lives. While I honestly still struggle with absences and cell phone use, the 17 Questions don't place students on the defensive (even though the questioning does sometimes confuse them, initially).

What has moved me regarding the questioning strategy is the mindset it requires you to adapt. You have to be curious about the student you are interviewing. You have to be open to what you are about to hear. You cannot condemn or judge because that would stop or ruin the conversation. It is essential that the teacher truly listens in order to keep the student talking. I want the student to talk; I want him or her to reveal something which will hopefully lead toward a transformation.

In the best case, the student feels better because of the interaction. In any case, the student has arrived at a point where it is not the teacher who is telling him/her to come to class or to turn in an assignment, it is solely the student coming to that conclusion.

I like learning about my students and it is such a bonus to have conversations become an impetus for change. Even if that change is a student knowing that I care to know just a little bit more.

Leighanne Law, Library and English

It is my first year at Scriber, and I absolutely love what I have seen and experienced. The school's culture is warm, supportive and extremely student-centered; I didn't know that schools like this existed in the public realm.

I was chatting with a student the other day about motivational interviewing. She asked, "Is it like jedi mind tricks?" and I said, "It's really just asking questions. Helping students get through tricky situations by reflecting and thinking deeply. It's about helping students take ownership, instead of telling them what to do." She and I agreed that "imparting" or telling people what to do never helps a situation, and that getting people to think for themselves actually makes change happen.

And it's true. It really does. I use these questions to deepen the thinking in my English class. I ask students these questions in passing. It is now so much a part of my lexicon, and so very helpful, that I can't imagine interacting with students in any other way.

Deb Walters, Counselor

The strength of Scriber has always been the one-on-one, caring and encouraging environment that we strive to provide. We have always wanted students to know that they are important and that they can be successful. The grant work has also added more framework so that more of the staff, a greater number of parents and the wider community are aware of our special niche.

For many alternative education students, the goal is to graduate, often without a vision for the future beyond high school. School is viewed as a place for earning credits and meeting requirements, rather than as a place of opportunity to acquire knowledge and skills that lead to successful adulthood. Many students in alternative programs say, "I don't like school and can hardly wait to get out. Why would I want more of it?" *Your Future Now* will change that.

Nathan Seright, Social Studies

During my short time at Scriber, I've noticed that students appear to enjoy coming to school. I like seeing them and they seem happy to speak with the teachers, too. This gives teachers the chance to check in with them and provides students with the opportunity to receive some emotional support for whatever is occurring in their lives. The staff are very invested in the students' success and in working together to support the school's mission. It really does seem a little like a family here.

Liza Behrendt, Leadership and Entry

We have become a kinder, gentler school since implementing the *Your Future Now* vision. I remember arriving as a paraeducator in early 2010. I had always wanted to work at an alternative high school, and I had hoped it would be a lively place where students were given second chances and lots of support. This was the case for sure, yet there was, in my perception, a sense of "us and them" woven into the school culture, coming from both staff and students. Sure, teachers were appreciated by students and vice versa. Graduation was a tearjerker for everyone, because by

June we, staff and students, had all gone through so much with each other. Still, there was not the same sense of being allied that I find today. Now it feels as though we are all on the same team.

I attribute this transformation to *Your Future Now*. From top administration through all levels of staff, I can feel a difference. Instead of seeing students as rascals that will get away with whatever they can, students are looked upon as gems in the rough, and our job is to help polish them to get to the shine.

The tone of staff meetings in the past was always caring towards students, but now there is an added element of considering, even more than before, what will happen in a given student's life after he or she graduates. Have we helped launch students' dreams? Have we nurtured skills that will lead to success? Have we fostered a sense of pride and accomplishment through abundant student mastery experiences?

In a sense, the educators at our school may feel more on the line than we did before, but that comes with deeper job satisfaction and greater engagement in the work itself. We get to respond to the hero's journey, the call for greatness, and that is soulful work.

Ann Paulson, *Your Future Now* Grant Evaluator and Focus Group Facilitator

Reflection on Teacher Focus Groups:

When I first walked in the doors of Scriber three years ago, I met a staff who was already intensely committed to the personal work of helping each student succeed. The list of barriers they faced was daunting. Most students were unmotivated and completely disconnected from education. Many faced heartbreakingly difficult circumstances. One teacher said "We are swimming upstream because they have had no successes; they are tuned out, turned off."

The first year, staff focused on changing conversations with students. Antagonism and discipline reduced. Teachers said "Being non-confrontational keeps my classes more focused and they sense that I am respecting them more" and "What I'm doing as a teacher is more meaningful." Still, many staff felt that this approach was "not right for all students."

By the end of the second year, staff had committed to a new way of working. From the classroom to the counseling center to the attendance office, Scriber staff began to speak the same language. New conversations had spurred on new policies and new curriculum. One teacher said, "It has changed the way I view education and it has changed my habits for the rest of my teaching career."

The grant is now wrapping up and Scriber is a different place. Yes, there are still barriers. Yes, there are still outcomes that need to be changed. More students need to make it to graduation. More students need to make it to college. However, the path forward has been lit; new conversations and the focus on the future have been institutionalized. New instructors and staff have come on board and stepped right into place. Staff, teachers and students are now working together to reach that future.

Reflection on Student Focus Groups:

In focus groups at the beginning of the grant, Scriber students agreed the school was a safety net, a last chance, a family for kids who may not have any. When asked what they were learning or how they'd use it after graduation, students started brainstorming like they'd never really thought about it before. Most students had one staff member he or she had connected with. Adults' expectations were generally to finish high school; graduation was the end game for all students. After graduation, almost half the students said they wanted to "take time off."

By the beginning of the third year, most students said they identified with many staff members across the school and the messages they were getting were about success in life. Students were very aware of their strengths. Every single student except one had college plans and most of them were very specific with the program and even the school selected. They'd really thought through the reasons for choosing the path they were on.

Marjie Bowker, English

Over the last three years of this grant work, I've experienced a series of "aha" moments that all add up to one significant transformation; I used to look for opportunities to leave my profession, but now I can't imagine doing anything else.

On an interpersonal level, I came to appreciate Cal's 17 Questions as "weapons of non-confrontation" —or as "17 ways to say 'I care about you.'" I've realized that the only reason I ever confronted a student before was because I lacked the tools to go another route. These questions allow a calm, curious, kind route that has relieved so much pressure from my work days. I've also realized that giving advice is rarely effective. We may have great intentions, but the best role we can possibly play is that of active listener and guide. Only the individual who has been through the actual experience has the power to decide how to take action. More pressure relieved.

Overall, the consciousness of our entire staff has risen significantly. Whether planning together or on our own, we now ask, "Is it meaningful? Is it a heart and soul activity? How do we strive for the transformation?" We no longer talk just of credits and graduation, but of purpose and dreams for the future. We all want to be engaged in something larger than ourselves, and that is what *Your Future Now* offers education. For three years, I have left our staff meetings full of excitement regarding my own future in this profession.

For all of these reasons, I knew that capturing and compiling our work was of the utmost importance; I didn't want our efforts and progress to disappear over time. And, as for the magic of writing, being intentional about collecting these conversations with students has served as a great reflective learning experience for all of us.

I'm so grateful to have had the support of a principal with a vision like Kathy Clift's, and I feel as though I have earned a degree in the Art of Asking and Listening from Cal Crow University.

My hope is that many educators will gain inspiration from this book, and that we will begin new conversations full of hope. If you're thinking, "My staff would never do this," I am pretty sure that Cal Crow would answer, "Well, what if they would?"

STAFF BIOS

Coley Armstrong has taught special education and history since 2012. He has worked for the Lake Washington District, and has been an employee of the Edmonds District for the past two years at Scriber (history, special education and entry) and in the Edmonds eLearning Academy (special education and history). Prior to his teaching career, Coley worked for Hertz Rent-A-Car for three years and served in the Army National Guard for six years, deploying to Iraq in support of Operation Iraqi Freedom III with 1-163rd INF, 116th Brigade Combat Team. Coley holds a bachelor's degree from the University of Montana and a master's in education from City University of Seattle.

Liza Behrendt began at Scriber in 2010, first as a paraeducator and career specialist. Her passion is helping people align their deepest truths with positive actions, to access and powerfully offer unique gifts to the world. Liza holds bachelor's degrees in women's studies and filmmaking, and master's degrees in transformative learning and teaching. Liza teaches leadership, interdisciplinary outdoor education and visual arts. She is the founding director of Beauty of Water (beautyofwater.org).

Marjie Bowker has taught English and a little history somewhere in the world for the past 18 years: in China, Norway and Vietnam, in addition to her "regular" spot at Scriber. She has published two curriculum guides: *They Absolutely Want to Write: Teaching the Heart and Soul of Narrative Writing* and *Hippie Boy Teaching Guide: Transforming Lives through Personal Storytelling.*

Carol Bowman moved from Utah to Washington as a young adult. She has worked at Troy Laundry, Seattle Tacoma Airport as a TSA officer, and Alfy's Pizza in Auburn as manager. She took business and art classes from Evergreen, Edmonds and Everett Community Colleges. She stayed at home to raise her two children in their early years, after which she served as a substitute in the Everett and Edmonds Districts. In 1998 she became the office manager at Scriber, where she continues to serve. She enjoys working with the students, hearing their stories and seeing their successes. She also enjoys gardening, hiking, and traveling.

Michael Carey has taught mathematics for the past ten years at the secondary level in the Edmonds School District, thriving in algebra and geometry at Scriber for the past eight years. He worked as an environmental geologist for 12 years prior to launching his teaching career. Mike enjoys hiking, bicycling, and paddling kayaks with his wife, Lenni.

Kathy Clift has served as principal of Scriber for 13 years and will retire this June after 40 years in education. Creating strategies that help students develop life-long goals and seeing them transform as they recognize their strengths has been the most rewarding part of her career. Her prior work includes an international teaching position in Australia and 23 years of teaching elementary and middle school in the Tahoma and Issaquah School Districts.

Cal Crow has been a teacher, counselor, university lecturer, consultant and trainer. He currently directs the Center for Efficacy and Resiliency at Edmonds Community College. He has consulted and trained throughout the United States and elsewhere on a variety of topics, all related to helping individuals create successful futures. He holds a Ph.D. from Arizona State University and is delighted to be part of Your Future Now.

Richard Croxon was born and raised in the inner city of Detroit, Michigan. He earned a Bachelor of Science with an honor citation in Psychology from Wayne State University and holds a master's in teaching from Seattle University. He also holds endorsements in general science and social studies. Besides teaching, Richard enjoys fishing and traveling.

Peter Folta has worked as a social studies teacher at Scriber since 2008. He began his career as an English teacher in 1995 at the American School in Hamburg, Germany. After returning to the U.S. he earned his master's in education from Seattle University in 2000. In 2012 he became a National Board Certified teacher, which prepared him well for *Your Future Now* work. He is active as a football and baseball coach in the community.

Brenna Hanson has been with Scriber since 2012 as the registrar in the counseling center. She enjoys working with all of the students and witnessing their transformations. Brenna holds a bachelor's in business administration with a concentration in human resource management from Western Washington University. She loves painting, photography, sports and hiking in the greater Seattle area.

Andrea Hillman has been an administrator at Scriber since early 2015. For the previous five years she served as an administrator at Meadowdale High School, and has administration experience in elementary and alternative high schools as well. Her career in education began as a Spanish teacher in 1998, following her family bloodline (her mother and a grandmother served in education as well). Her travels have taken her to five continents, and she has hosted upwards of 10 student trips overseas. Andrea taught in Spain, and earned a master's at the University of Salamanca. She was born and raised in Mountain, ND (population 134), and is proud of her Icelandic heritage. She is honored to have been selected to be the next principal of Scriber, and is excited to see how *Your Future Now* can continue to impact students' lives.

Barb Kathol has been greeting everyone at Scriber's attendance office since 2005. She feels fortunate to have the opportunity to listen to all the stories that students and staff share, and her goal is to have an answer for every question asked. Prior to Scriber, Barb was a "stay at home" mom raising two children. She attended the University of Washington in the early 1970's and then traveled around Europe for six months. She worked in Nordstrom's Store Planning department for 12 years as a purchasing agent and buyer for the interiors of the new stores, traveling via the Nordstrom Learjet.

Greg Lange has been in education since 1990. The universe sent students to him at that point as a gift, shortly after he decided to get sober following a 15-year career of self-inflicted spiritual and physical toxicity. His first job in education was as a middle school day-shift custodian where he discovered that he could garner student respect, even as students faced adversity and significant challenges. After 20+ years, there is rarely a day when coming to work, especially at Scriber, is not a true joy for Greg. When people say, "Honor your passion when finding a job," he feels that they are right!

Leighanne Law is a first-year teacher-librarian and English teacher. Her passion is connecting young people to amazing books, and through those amazing books, the world. Before earning a master's in teaching from the University of Washington in 2014, she was a children's and young adult bookseller for nine years at three different bookstores: McLean & Eakin in Michigan, Phinney Books and The Elliott Bay Book Company in Seattle. She is currently working on completing her School Library Media endorsement through the University of Washington.

Paula Lott began her career in a San Francisco inner city school upon earning teaching certification at San Francisco State University. After teaching for several years, she took time off to raise a family. During that time she was involved in leadership roles in Girl Scouts and the community. Born in Berkeley California, she has lived in five different states, staying active within schools, Girl Scouts and the community in each location. She joined the Scriber staff in 2002, teaching subjects within Family and Consumer Science.

Trinity Meriwood earned a bachelor's in business and marketing at Seattle University as a three-sport athlete on a soccer scholarship. After experiencing the corporate environment for a few years she decided in 2001 to change to education. She earned a Bachelor of Science degrees in Business Education and in Marketing Education from Central Washington University, where she played rugby and was an assistant coach for the fast pitch softball team. In 1996 she joined the Army Reserves, then switched to the Washington Army National Guard, through which she deployed to Iraq for Operation Iraqi Freedom. At Scriber she shares her background in graphic design, honed through promoting events as a DJ. Her students design projects throughout the school, including the cover for Scriber students' latest book, *We Hope You Rise*.

Kristi Myers began her career in the Midwest working in psychiatric hospitals with adolescents struggling with behavioral and mental health issues. She entered the field of education after obtaining a master's degree at the University of Washington in special education with a focus on emotional and behavioral disorders. She joined the staff at Scriber in the fall of 2014 to lead the intensive learning support program.

Ann Paulson is currently on the faculty at Edmonds Community College. Her focus has been on closing the opportunity gap; she believes education, graduation, and career success should be available to everyone and has worked for the last six years as an evaluator for grants focused on that goal. Ann volunteers for 501 Commons as a strategic planning consultant for nonprofits, especially youth development organizations. She holds a Ph.D. from the University of Nebraska, Lincoln. Go Huskers!

Sarah Philley began at Scriber in 2002, serving in various roles until becoming the Competency Based Learning (CBL) coordinator. Sarah credits her own graduation in the midst of an unstable home life to the positive support she received from her alternative high school staff, community, and colleagues in Maple Valley; she aims to offer the same support to local youth. Currently completing a master's in community psychology, Sarah holds bachelor's degrees in education, psychology, and social justice. She is passionate about providing experiential opportunities that enhance community ties, career exploration, and life skills. Sarah developed Experiencing Seattle: From Failing to Thriving, and is the founding executive director of Thrive City (fromfailingtothriving.com).

Nate Seright is one of the newest additions to the Scriber staff. He has been an educator since 2002 when he graduated from the University of North Dakota. He has worked with students in all grades and many different subjects, but he loves teaching history the most. In the past he has worked in the areas of service learning, English as a foreign language, and project-based learning. Recently he returned to the U.S. after six years of teaching in South Korea. His best experiences with students have been in the small school setting where genuine, supportive relationships are possible.

Tammy Stapleton has been working for the Edmonds District since 1998. For the first several years she worked in various positions as a classified substitute, then became a 1:1 paraeducator in Learning Support at Mountlake Terrace High School in 2004. Since 2010 she has been working in the Student Transition Education Program (STEP) at Scriber. She grew up in Kentucky and has lived in Bothell with her husband since 1987. They have three children.

Zach Taylor is in his second year at Scriber, now serving as the Career and College Specialist. For five years he has been a track and football coach at Lynnwood and Meadowdale High Schools in the Edmonds District, and is currently working on a masters in teaching. Zach is in his dream job at Scriber; working with kids has always been his life's passion. He has also worked as an English teacher in China, an advocate for homeless youth in Seattle, and in the culinary industry. In his free time Zach enjoys traveling to new places via foot or bicycle with his fiancée, Sarah.

Sondra Thornton is a paraeducator who came to Scriber in 2009, having served in the Edmonds District since 2001, originally at the elementary level. She chose Scriber because she was drawn to the population and knew many of the students, including her daughter. Another daughter later came to Scriber because she had been bullied elsewhere. Both daughters are now in technical colleges. Sondra is the proud mother of five, grandmother of 13, and great grandmother of four and counting!

Kanoe Vierra has taught high school English in the Edmonds District for the past 12 years, serving at Scriber for the past eight years, including as Dean of Students. Kanoe believes that every student has strengths, skills and talents to be discovered and developed, and that all students can have the future they dream of. Kanoe worked in the healthcare industry for 22 years prior to teaching. A former wrestler himself, he was head coach at Mountlake Terrace High School, where his team won numerous team and individual academic awards. Kanoe enjoys reading, building furniture, fishing, bicycling, and spending time with his wife, Cheryl, family, and beloved grandchildren.

Michael Waldren is a teacher assistant at Scriber. After providing his services to IT companies in eastern Washington for half a year, he realized that he missed education, and returned to help students succeed. Previously a substitute in the State of Florida, Michael aims to make clear to all students that absolutely nothing is academically out of reach, and to never let anybody say otherwise. Michael is a history scholar and has plans to amplify his ambitions in historiography and writing.

Lynn Willman holds a master's of education degree from Seattle University. She has been a school counselor for nearly 18 years, all at Scriber. Lynn is passionate about working with people who are learning to enjoy learning, discovering their gifts, building their skills and thinking about where their knowledge, strengths, and skills intersect with passions. Along with her husband, Lynn is the parent of three amazing teenagers and is excited about how their journeys are unfolding. Lynn enjoys food: growing it, baking it, cooking it, and eating it; she also loves anything that gets her outside, the beauty of the Northwest and travel.

Richard Yi, a Seattle native, holds a bachelor's in mathematics from the University of Washington and a master's in mathematics education from Teachers College Columbia University in New York City. In 2006 he was selected as one of the ten teaching fellows in the Urban Teaching Fellowship program, through which he had the opportunity to teach math for one year at a public middle school in New York City. After completing the program he relocated to the Seattle area and has been teaching middle and high school math in both public and private schools since 2007. Richard has been teaching algebra and geometry at Scriber since January of 2015.

David Zwaschka has taught English over the last 25 years in Alaska, Tennessee, North Carolina and Washington, with moments of administration in between. His first year at Scriber has been a revelation, and he is looking forward to continuing his work with Scriber's terrific students and dedicated staff. Dave enjoys running, reading, hiking in the North Cascades and not having any pets. He and his wife, Claire, have two teenage daughters.

FURTHER READING

Self-efficacy:

Self-efficacy: An Essential Motive to Learn

Barry J. Zimmerman, City University of New York: Contemporary Educational Psycyhology, 25, 82-91 (2000)

Resiliency:

Resiliency: What We Have Learned

Bonnie Benard, WestEd, A Trade Paper (2004)

Fostering Resiliency in Kids: Protective Factors in the Family, School, and Community

Far West Research Laboratory for Educational Research and Development (2004)

Appreciative Inquiry:

Leadership at Every Level: Appreciative Inquiry in Education

Rich Henry, New Horizons for Learning (2003)

A Positive Revolution in Change: Appreciative Inquiry

David L. Cooperrider, Case Western Reserve University; Diana Whitney, The Taos Institute

A Strengths-Based Whole System Approach

Gina Hinrichs, Appreciative Inquiry Commons (2002)

Motivational Interviewing:

Facilitating Change: Using Motivational Interviewing Techniques to Help Young People Understand their Behaviour

Atkinson, Cathy, Sodapop CD ROM (2005)